For Lester William Polfus

'Great for budding rockers - a great
reference item for when your Les
Paul needs a little extra'

Vintage Guitar

First published in September 2008
Reprinted December 2009

A catalogue record for this book is available from the British
Library

ISBN 978 1 84425 478 1

Library of Congress catalog card no. 2008926349

Published by Haynes Publishing,
Sparkford, Yeovil, Somerset BA22 7JJ, UK

Tel: 01963 442030 Fax: 01963 440001
Int. tel: +44 1963 442030 Int. fax: +44 1963 440001
E-mail: sales@haynes.co.uk
Website: www.haynes.co.uk

Haynes North America, Inc.,
861 Lawrence Drive, Newbury Park,
California 91320, USA

Printed and bound in the UK

Haynes

Gibson
Les Paul

Manual

Includes Epiphone models

Haynes Publishing

Haynes

Gibson
Les Paul
Manual
Includes Epiphone models

**How to buy, maintain
and set up the legendary
Les Paul electric guitar**

Paul Balmer
Foreword by Les Paul

Contents

Foreword by Les Paul

I first started experimenting with a solid body guitar in the late '20s. I'd already cannibalised my mother's telephone to amplify my voice and harmonica, but a customer complained they couldn't hear the guitar. So I went to work on this. But just amplifying the guitar with a phonograph pickup produced a lot of acoustic feedback, so I tried stuffing the guitar with rags to reduce this. Eventually I filled it with plaster of Paris!

My experiments continued much later at the Epiphone factory in New York – basically adding experimental guitar pickups to a piece of 4x4 timber. This worked fine but everybody laughed. People listen with their eyes you know. So I attached a couple of guitar bouts to the 'log' and everybody was happy.

However, none of the guitar makers could see the potential for the idea until in 1950 my friend Leo Fender came up with his 'canoe paddle' – he gave me one incidentally, which I still have – never been played. I was committed to a Gibson or Epiphone type guitar like the wonderful L5s I have from 1929–30 or my serial number 6867 Epiphone with the useful 'trapdoor' in the back. This 'Klunker' was great as I could continually experiment with different pickups and 'pots' without ripping the guitar apart. I had three Klunkers in all, so I could keep one as a reference point and experiment on the others.

So when Gibson finally came back to me in 1951 I had lots of ideas for a solid electric guitar. I still got my first two Les Pauls and they're the two best guitars I've got.

I'm pleased the guitar that bears my name has proved so popular. It works fine, just needs a little love and attention once in a while, like any gal.

Try to be a good person and have a good time doing it.

Lester William Polfus
September 2008

Introduction

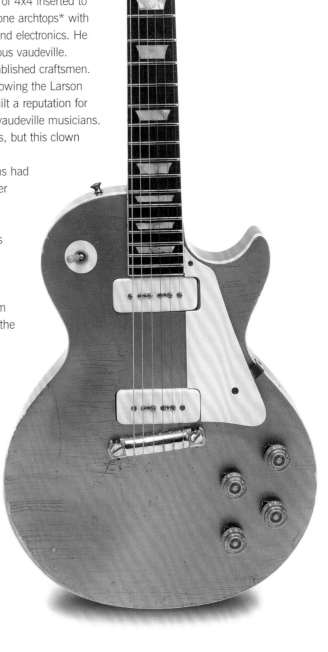

Lester William Polfus, aka 'Rhubarb Red', first took the audacious idea of a solid body electric guitar to Gibson Guitars in 1946.

Visionary inventor and musician Polfus had realised the limitations of merely fitting an electric pickup to a conventional archtop acoustic guitar as early as 1941. With Les Paul as his adopted stage name, his fame was soon enough for him to be allowed the run of the New York Epiphone factory at West 14th Street at weekends. These experimental sessions produced the 'Logs' – acoustic guitars hacked in half and a solid piece of 4x4 inserted to hold the pickups. His experiments also produced his 'Klunkers', Epiphone archtops* with trapdoors in the back to facilitate interchanging experimental pickups and electronics. He took these experimental guitars to Gibson, who laughed at this audacious vaudeville.

To put this in perspective, by 1946 the Gibson company were established craftsmen. Founded in 1894 under the initial guidance of Orville Gibson and following the Larson Brothers' introduction of louder, more robust steel strings, they had built a reputation for revolutionary carved top 'orchestral' guitars for dance band, jazz and vaudeville musicians. They had tolerated the addition of pickups to their hand-carved guitars, but this clown Polfus was clearly going too far!

However, by 1950 things were changing. Western Swing musicians had quickly realised the benefits of Leo Fender's 'canoe paddle' Broadcaster guitars, and the call went out from Gibson/CMI boss Maurice Berlin, 'Find that guy with the broomstick!'

This resulted in the *other* iconic guitar of popular music, which sits alongside and perfectly complements the Fender Stratocaster.

Unlike the Stratocaster, however, the Les Paul lacked a production test bed. By 1954 Leo Fender had learned a lot from his Esquire, Broadcaster and Telecaster guitars, and discerning players had fed him all the clues he needed. Despite last-minute hitches with the vibrato, the 1954 Strat was almost an Immaculate Conception.

The 1952 'Les Paul' in contrast was almost a disaster. As we shall see, the original bridge was unworkable, as was the neck tilt; and, most importantly, the classic-sounding 'humbuckers' – the dinosaur voice of the Les Paul – *were yet to be invented*. Fortunately, however, the guitar looked cool, and Les Paul was himself inventor enough to fix some of these problems on the guitars that he was soon seen playing on TV and recording with in his home studio.

According to Lester the first tune recorded on a prototype

*The three archtop Epiphone klunkers are serial numbers 6867, 4108 and 7133. Significantly they were played in 1946 by Django Reinhardt and Johnny Smith, and remain in Lester's possession in 2008. He had three klunkers because he kept one as a scientific 'control' reference whilst constantly experimenting on the others. Most of Les Paul's hits were recorded on the klunkers.

Gibson Les Paul was the traditional jazz classic *Tiger Rag*, recorded by Lester in winter 1951/2. This seems an appropriate repertoire for what was effectively a small 'solid' but otherwise traditional archtop jazz guitar. Significantly this was quickly followed by two 'blues', *Deep In The Blues* and *St Louis Blues* in summer and winter 1952. It's spooky to listen to these tracks and hear shades of Chuck Berry as Lester bends adjacent 1st and 2nd strings into a familiar de-tuned unison – in its first year the hybrid guitar had found its most familiar voice.

Innovations that *did* stand the test of time were already present in the '52 opus. Gibson were traditionalists, and they rightly felt that a carved maple top was their signature – their *guitar* was not to be a 'plank' or a canoe paddle. Consequently The Les Paul started out $20 more expensive than a 'Tele'.

With notable exceptions, the marrying of a solid plank of mahogany to a carved maple top remains a distinct signature of the literally 'Heavy' Les Paul sound.

The scale length is also significant. Gibson chose from the outset a 24.75in scale, slightly shorter than Fender's 25.5in working string length – though the significance this would have for easier and more subtle 'string bending' by later blues exponents would only be fully exploited post-1966.

Though Les Paul rarely played a Goldtop himself, reckoning that black looked cooler with a tuxedo, the 'Goldtop' finish *was* his idea: 'Gold means rich, expensive, the best, superb.'

Appropriately for an inventor's instrument, the Les Paul guitar continues to evolve, with 'Digital' and 'Robot' versions alongside classic Goldtops and 'bursts.

Les Paul

Born in Waukesha, Wisconsin, in 1915, Les Paul is a true genius, one of the greatest innovators in the history of popular music. The guitar that bears his name is an icon seen on every stage and screen and heard on millions of records. Lester's own story is a walking, talking, guitar-slinging romp through the history of American popular music.

He first recorded in Chicago in 1936, accompanying black blues singer Georgia White. He later played with artists as diverse as Django Reinhardt, Nat King Cole and Charlie Christian, achieving his ambition of replacing Eddie Lang as guitarist to the first 'pop star', Bing Crosby, in 1945. In the 1950s he had many number one chart successes with singer Colleen Summers, working as popular duo 'Les Paul & Mary Ford'.

The Les Paul Gibson is the guitar he began to visualise in the 1930s and '40s and cajoled and inspired Gibson luthiers to finally develop during 1951.

Back in the '30s Lester had cannibalised his mother's telephone to obtain a microphone for his early performances. I asked Lester how this early amplification was received by the audience:

'Playing an early gig a fella sent a note via the car hop saying that singing on the telephone mike and playing harmonica was fine, but the only thing that wasn't loud enough was *the guitar*, and that sent me home that night concerned about making the guitar louder. This was about 1930. I had my guitar and harmonica hooked up to my mom's radio and my guitar plugged into my dad's phonograph, but the feedback problem was terrible.

'So by taking an acoustic guitar and filling it full of rags, socks, shorts and a tablecloth I partially got rid of some feedback problems. I then filled it full of plaster of Paris and that got rid of more. But it didn't take me but a second longer to figure out that there's only one way to properly do it, and that's to find something that would *restrict any other movement other than the string!*

'It had to be like a railroad track that was not going to contribute any other sounds, just the string vibrating, and if I placed a pickup, which was made of telephone parts, underneath it then I would get the exact sound of the string of the guitar. *Where* I placed it under the string was a matter of choice of harmonics.

'I made a prototype out of a soft piece of wood that would simulate a guitar and contribute many resonant sounds or colourations to the sound. The other prototype was literally a railroad track, which contributed nothing, and placing the two side by side in no time at all I figured that what I was looking for was a railroad track! In practical terms, however, I found out that a four by four inch timber is OK if you're trying to make a solid body instrument. So I finally devised a way of making a four by four look like a guitar – when I tried the guitar without the conventional sides bolted on nobody responded; people listen with their eyes, you know!

'I took it to the different companies and they all laughed at it. No one took it seriously.'

Pickups

'There are several harmonics in a guitar that are much lower than other harmonics, so it's a question of personal taste in pickup positioning, like putting salt into food, how much salt you wish to put in. If you're positioning at the bridge then you have a choice of getting almost everything, including a lot of things that you don't wish!

'Western Electric deserves a lot of credit for keeping me on the right track. I imagine it had to be the early 1920s that I took my mother's telephone and took the receiver to find out what the impedance was of the coils, and they were humbucked at that time! And that turned out to be exactly what I wanted. I heard the sound I wanted to hear.

'I used the receiver part for the pickup – that is, the magnet and the coil. The part that you speak into was a carbon microphone. I also used the carbon mike to sing into, so Western Electric deserves a lot of credit!

'Even the "Log"* guitar pickups are very simple – I used a magnet and a coil and that was it. I didn't want to add anything to change anything from its original state. I had to wind them myself, though!'

Eventually, as Leo Fender's guitar began to make an impact Lester was invited to collaborate with Gibson on the development and promotion of an electric solid body guitar. I asked him about the origin of the distinctive Les Paul carved top:

'When I went to Gibson I made the suggestion of a *flat* top, and the chairman of the board asked me "Do you like violins?" I said, "Well I love violins." And he said "Well I have a vault full of them, I collect violins." And he showed me and I was quite impressed with his collection. But what he was really telling me was "Wouldn't you like to have an archtop on the guitar like the violin's?" And I said "I would have gone there in a second, but I figured it cost so much more to shape the top of the guitar than a flat top." And he said "Forget the cost of it. The fact is that we're prepared to do that, we have the tools, that would be an act of Gibson." *That* was their contribution to that guitar for me.

'Knowing that it was going to be more like a gal, or more like your wife, it made it more beautiful. And the one thing I wanted to make out of the guitar was a beautiful instrument, not a plank of wood with some gears on it!

'I just have the one flat-top Les Paul, which I take down to the club once in a while and compare it with what's going on now and the changes over the years. And there are no changes, so as far as the archtop versus the flat top, it doesn't change the *sound* of the instrument.

'The sound is coming mostly from the *neck* of the guitar. The neck is the most important part of that guitar, and that will resonate, and that will give you the characteristic sound – *not what you want*, but that's what you're stuck with. It's a fact that you have to have a neck on the guitar. Things like that aren't advantageous, they're actually *colouring* the sound. Ideally you'd like the railroad track with no colouration, you'd like the string to vibrate by itself.

'For the neck we went to ebony, which is a very hard wood. And then there are those that preferred a warm sound and wanted the colouration that was gotten from a piece of rosewood, for instance, *and the customer's always right!* So, if that's what they wished, that's what they got. I don't go round with a book in my hand to tell them how comparisons are made, I give them what they want. And that's how we learn; as they learn.'

Guitar summit

'Leo Fender was a very good friend of mine until he passed away – we were very good friends. We talked about everything quite a bit. In California sometimes there would be me, Leo and Paul Bigsby, all in the backyard discussing the solid body guitar – why he liked a certain thing, and how many things we both liked, and how we were to accomplish what we accomplished. Those brain sessions changed the world.'

The original 'Trapeze' tailpiece

'The trapeze tailpiece on the '52 was made for an archtop, and that led to the stop bar, which eliminated all the contraption behind the tailpiece and made it much simpler. Most of these things are just practical. If you sit there looking at them you're going to figure them out.'

EQ and onboard electronics

'If you make a guitar and it's right, then you shouldn't need extreme things on it. The amplifier tomorrow – I believe this – will be "flat". That'll be it! If there's any equalisation that's used there it's to fit the room that you're in, because when you take your amplifier and place it in different rooms it's going to sound different…'

I asked if, looking back on the guitar generally, there was anything he would change in a perfect world?

'Yeah, the tuning! Somehow we got this unorthodox tuning and learned to live with it!

'We started at the beginning and we were pioneering this thing through its infancy. There's so much to learn, and this was exciting, interesting, and there was so much room. When you leave the ground there's so much out there!'

(This is an edited version of an interview given by Lester William Polfus – then aged 92 – to Paul Balmer in August 2007.)

*See page 152 for more on the 'Log' electric guitar prototypes.

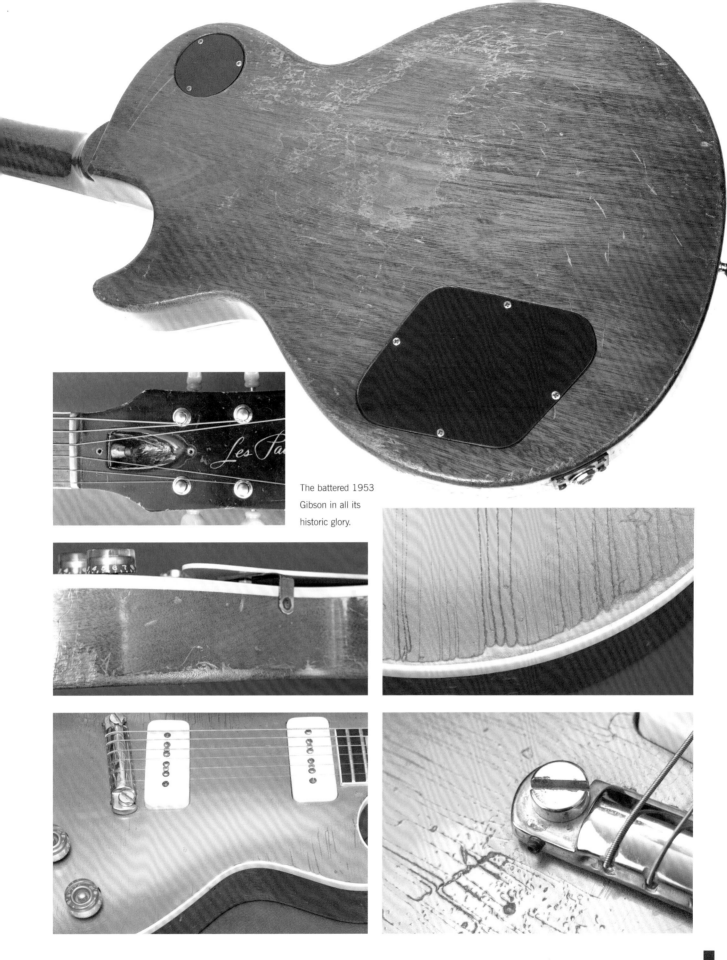

The battered 1953 Gibson in all its historic glory.

A classic 'Standard'

Though the Les Paul guitar first appeared in 1952 it wasn't until 1957 that the 'Standard'* acquired its rightly famous Seth Lover 'Patent Applied For' double coil 'humbucking' pickups.

When musicians enthuse about the Les Paul guitar they usually mean *this* model, and from 1958 onwards they rightly crave this distinct but accidental faded sunburst finish. Though the '52 Goldtop was the first 'Les Paul' guitar, the 'Standard' – which first came to prominence with Eric Clapton in 1966 – became the iconic blues and rock guitar.

1,712 is simply a number. But in the guitar world it's *the* number – the number of Les Paul 'Standards' Gibson produced between 1958 and 1960. All 1,712 were made by a small community of 12 craftsmen working at the Gibson factory at 225 Parson Street, Kalamazoo. In 1958 the 'Standard' cost $247 and 50 cents!

*The 'Standard' name was not officially used by Gibson until 1960.

Body The body of a true Les Paul is a unique blend of solid mahogany capped with a carved maple top. This gives the guitar its shape and its natural sustain. There are 'solid' mahogany Les Pauls, but they have a different sonic signature (*see page 120, the Les Paul 'Custom'*).

Tune-O-Matic bridge A refinement of the Melita brothers' design, the Tune-O-Matic arrived on the Les Paul 'Custom' in 1954 and the 'Regular' in 1955, and enabled accurate adjustment of intonation only rivalled by the '54 Fender Stratocaster (*see page 78*).

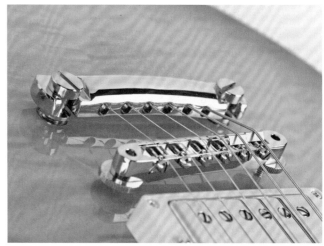

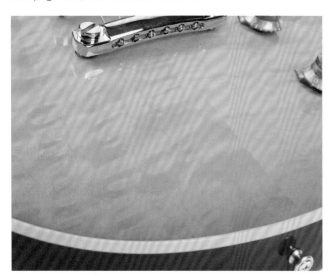

Neck Made of mahogany and with a shorter scale length than solid body rivals Fender, the Les Paul had a rosewood or ebony fingerboard from the outset. Perhaps the most important facet is the glued in 'set' neck with a traditional 'long tenon' set into the body – harder to repair than a 'bolt-on' neck but with potential for more 'uncoloured' string sustain (*see page 74*).

Separate pickguard Often missing in action. The Les Paul has a traditional separate pickguard – a carry-over from Gibson's 'cello guitars' – but with a new rocket tailfin shape redolent of 1950s Science Fiction.

Humbucking pickups These revolutionary pickups were designed by Seth Lover to cancel inducted hum. However, by accident they became famous for their louder, mellower audio character. Most importantly their higher electrical output more easily overloads the front end of a valve amplifier – the birth of 'The Bluesbreaker' *(see page 156)*.

Tone and volume controls A direct analogy of their radio origins, these primitive resistive capacitive circuits do the job.

Wide frets Though not on the early Les Pauls, Gibson generally advocates the potential lower action and possible sonic benefits of wider 'chunkier' fret wire. As ever, most Les Pauls have a distinctive bound fingerboard.

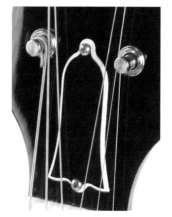

Accessible truss rod Invented for their banjos by Gibson's Thadeus McHugh in 1922, this truss rod is accessible by the removal of two screws and a plastic cover *(see page 98)*. This was a clear advantage over 1950s Fenders, which at this time still required part disassembly for truss rod adjustment.

Kluson-type machine heads with distinctive decorative 'tulip' heads. John Kluson supplied these fairly efficient if rather primitive 1938 patented machines. They are currently still used on some Les Pauls, technically improved if aesthetically similar.

Pickup selector A simple three-way toggle provides neck bridge for both pickups. The Rhythm/Treble markings are a refinement not found on the '52 guitar.

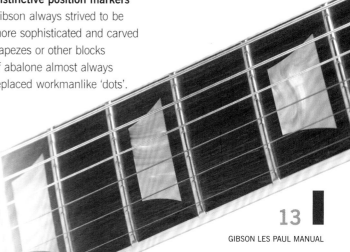

Distinctive position markers Gibson always strived to be more sophisticated and carved trapezes or other blocks of abalone almost always replaced workmanlike 'dots'.

Buying a Les Paul

The beginning of the 21st century is a fantastic time to buy a Les Paul. The choice has never been better. At Sothebys millionaires can bid for 'Greeny', Peter Green's legendary '59 Sunburst, and working guitarists can buy a virtually identical guitar on the Internet or the High Street for a few months' salary. For a week's wages beginners can acquire a workmanlike look-alike from Epiphone, and those with an eye on the future can check out an Ethernet-ready 'Digital' Les Paul or a 'Robot' Les Paul that even tunes itself.

LEFT A Bigsby-equipped 'Custom'.

RIGHT An Epiphone Goldtop '56 reissue.

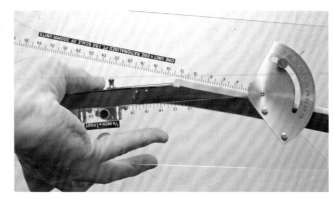

Correct authentic 17° headstock pitch.

■ Epiphone 'Standards', 'Customs' and Goldtops

The Epiphone range is made by parent company Gibson specifically to cater for the beginner and budget-conscious guitarist. The Epiphone marque has a history and kudos of its own, only slightly sullied by a rash of ill-conceived budget guitars in the late 20th century.

Now made chiefly in China, these look-alikes are improving all the time. Often the only overt giveaway to their budget source is the distinctive Epiphone headstock, which is subtly different from the classic Gibson contour but no less attractive.

The sound can be very impressive, especially if higher spec pickups are retro-fitted (*see page 80*). As with any guitar the key playability and intonation factor is a good set-up (*see page 34*).

Definitive stop tail and Tune-O-Matic bridges (except '52 reissue).

■ The Les Paul Collection

Gibson now offer over a dozen variants on this design classic. These can be supplied in approaching 20 different finishes. The collection ranges from microscopically correct emulations of the golden age '58–'60 'bursts to futuristic seven-string and digital tools for new music.

The new Gibsons have certain features in common:

Modern machine heads of either vintage or current outward appearance.

BurstBuckers or P90 type pickups offering PAF or overwound options.

Standard 'Honeyburst' '60 neck
An affordable working guitar with a vintage vibe.

Les Paul Quilt Top 'Standard'
From their custom catalogue, something very like a '59 Les Paul with a few modern touches.

'Vintage Original Spec' series
Made in the Gibson custom shop these guitars strive to exactly emulate the classic Les Pauls. The details involved in this venture mean there are dedicated models for each year '56–'60 in 'Standard', 'Custom' and Goldtop models. This is as close as you can currently get to owning a Vintage Les Paul without taking on a second mortgage.

Artist Collection
In this series Gibson offer a Jimmy Page Les Paul, a Joe Perry, a Peter Frampton, and a Slash, as well as a growing collection of new artists.

Gibson Custom Shop 'Black Beauty'
The Gibson custom shop offers such rarities as a '54 Goldtop and a two-pickup 'Black Beauty' – basically anything you can afford!

Les Paul Standard 'Faded' and 'Supreme'
No wear and tear, but all the 'fade' alongside 'The Ultimate Les Paul', with all the trimmings and the finest maple.

Les Paul Studios
No frills, unbound, thinner and lighter but otherwise a classic. Lots of finishes including white. The guitars incorporate swamp ash and muiricatiera woods alongside the traditional maple and mahogany.

'Digital' and 'Robot'
The classic Les Paul guitar with bonus features. Six discrete digital pickups, one for each string, or automatic retuning to custom pitches of your choice – the future in cool blue.

With second-hand Les Pauls changing hands for £150,000 ($275,000) the buyer must beware. The golden era Les Paul 'Standards' of '58–'60 are the Holy Grail of guitar collectors, and unscrupulous fakers are at work. If you are offered a rare guitar at a knockdown price it's probably stolen. Eric Clapton's 'Bluesbreaker' guitar is still on the missing list.

Also bear in mind that only a very experienced expert can tell which elements of a presented guitar are real. As with any mass-produced product, many of the parts have been available in various forms over the last 50-plus years so there are many 'bitsa' Les Pauls out there – 'bits a this, and bits a that' – Slash played one for years to great effect.

A trusted, respected dealer or auction house is a good place to start.

Some issues to address when buying second-hand

■ Corrosion of metal parts
This is generally not a huge problem unless you are primarily concerned over aesthetics. But bridges do rust, and this can hamper intonation adjustments. The same applies to machine heads. However, good authentic-looking replacements are easily available. (See *Useful contacts* appendix.)

■ Fret and fingerboard wear
Fortunately the Les Paul has always had a separate fingerboard, so a re-fret – whilst expensive due to the replacement/repair of the binding – is perfectly possible. Be careful whom you trust to do this and consult authorities such as the American Society of Luthiers for recommendations. A skilled craftsman will always use the appropriate 'period' fretwire on a rare and valuable instrument.

■ Pickups

The original PAF pickups are the most coveted in the guitar world so if your guitar has them *keep them*. If they're broken a re-wind is possible. Authentic coil wire and turning figures are available from expert sources.

■ Noisy tone and volume pots

These are easily replaced – keep the originals as a source of provenance (see boxout at right). *See page 84* regarding replacing a volume pot.

■ Missing parts

Often old Gibsons have lost some peripherals; control knobs, machine heads and pickup covers are the most common. These are all now available and can even be supplied 'aged' to preserve vintage cool.

■ Authenticity

Serial numbers for vintage Les Pauls are a confusing minefield and the manufacture of so many period look-alikes at different times means you must consult a very experienced luthier or fellow collector.

My honest advice *to a player* at this stage in the development of the electric guitar is: buy new. There has never been such a rich diversity of choice. To my ears the new guitars sound as good if not better, and the manufacturing tolerances are now computer-controlled, ensuring that all the engineering aspects of Les Pauls have never been better. The faded magnetism of a '59 PAF pickup may have charm but without Peter Green's genius a pickup is sadly just a bunch of wires.

Verifying authenticity

Seek provenance, as you would with any 'antique'. The Sothebys commissioned expert will seek the telltale signs of cloth-covered push-back wires and aged wax. Paint formulae are also forensically verifiable.

Seek also any documentation – 'hang tags', original cases and photographs of alleged vintage wonders in dateable stage situations. Pot codes are a useful cross-reference. *See the pot codes appendix, page 168.*

The greatest irony is that a year of issue '52 Les Paul in original condition would be declared unworkable by Les Paul himself, so without extensive 'modernisation' would remain a curio. This is due to issues such as neck pitch and trapeze tailpieces *(see page 78)*.

Know your classic Goldtop '53

Due to a misunderstanding between Les Paul and the Gibson design team, a few Goldtops were produced in the first year of manufacture with a disastrous 'wrap-under' trapeze bridge. However, the 'de-bugged' Goldtop of 1953 is a rock'n'roll classic. Every part proclaims it a thoroughbred. Unlike its rivals this was no 'parts guitar'; it exuded craftsmanship and the luthier's hand. Gibson were clearly replying to Leo Fender's 'canoe paddle' Telecaster with a guitar that sat comfortably within their tradition.

LEFT Note the very 'flat' top.

RIGHT The holy grail?

This guitar's success can be measured in sales figures: by the mid 1950s electric guitars accounted for over 65 per cent of Gibson sales. The Goldtop was originally offered in 1952 at $210.

For me the guitar is forever part of the image of electric pioneers Freddie King and Carl Perkins: *'You can keep the blue suede shoes – just lay off my guitar'*.

■ Frets

Originally the Les Paul 'Regular' carried 22 very thin, almost mandolin-width frets mounted on an unbound rosewood fingerboard. However, this example has been re-fretted with a more blues-friendly 'chunky' variety. Lester has had the same adjustment made to his original prototype.

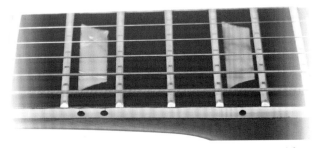

This '53 guitar has a bound fingerboard with no jagged fret edges to catch a player's hand – *not* a feature on the very first '52s.

but *we* at Gibson make guitars!' Interestingly Les Paul himself prefers his personal guitars with a flat top! This ties in with his personal style of playing – a flurry of fast staccato rather than long, smooth, overdriven sustain. This '53 has a comparatively flat carved top – 50mm less height than is common on the 'classic' late '50s Les Paul.

■ Wrap-over bridge

The disastrous trapeze bridge of '52 would finally, in 1954, evolve into the solution found on the 'Custom' Les Paul – the combination of a solid anchor stop tail and the newly patented Gibson Tune-O-Matic bridge. The depicted 'part solution' arrived on the Goldtop in 1953, the 'wrap-over' giving the strings the stability required to complement the maple top's inherent sustain and allowing the player to use palm muting. The bridge has some crude adjustment for string length.

■ Single cutaway

Gibson had no way of predicting the Stratocaster's 'double-cut' emergence in the following year, so the Kalamazoo designers followed the single-cut pattern of their own ES175 and Leo Fender's Telecaster. In practice the single cut provides adequate playability.

■ Carved top

This feature really set the Les Paul apart. It not only defines the guitar's sound but it redefines the Gibson 'archtop' guitar – Orville Gibson's seminal invention. It's tantamount to saying 'Those dammed radio spares guys in California can saw a plank

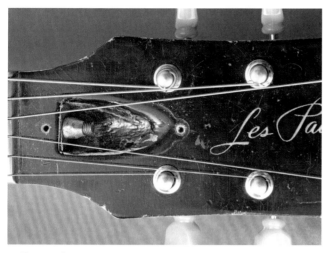

■ Gold lacquer

The striking finish of the new guitar was achieved through multiple lustrous coats of nitro-cellulose lacquer on a maple base. Most Goldtops are just that, gold on top with mahogany natural finish on the back and sides. However, there are a few rare examples from circa 1955 that are all gold. For Les Paul gold meant 'wealth, riches – the best!' This finish was adapted from the earlier archtop ES 295.

The gold lacquer does tend to shrink and crack.

■ Truss rod

From the outset the Les Paul came fitted with a usable, easily accessible truss rod. This metal rod inserted along the length of the neck both counteracted the natural tendency of a wooden neck to bend under string tension and offered a simple solution to correcting any concave

tendency that did occur. This was particularly pertinent in the 1950s, when strings came in two gauges, *heavy* and *extra heavy*. The truss rod adjustment has always been aesthetically disguised by a 'shield', often bearing a name or logo – 'Les Paul' being one option, not yet implemented in '53.

■ P90s

The single coil 'soapbar' P90s are the heart of the Goldtop. They sound grittier and are more mid-frequency biased than Fender's single coils, and have a grunt in their voice that gave character to many early electric Chicago and Texas blues. The neck pickup DC resistance measured on this example is a very low 7.76K ohms and the bridge at 7.45K ohms. The P90s were not developed specifically for this guitar but adapted from previous hollow archtop guitar pickups dating to as early as 1946.

■ Elaborate fret markers

Very early Les Pauls are found without neck binding but always with fancy inlays to mark the most significant frets. These are most often trapezoid, but block oblongs appear on early 'Customs'. From the beginning the Les Paul had a sense of a little old world luxury. The 'crown' shape inlays had first appeared on the 1950 ES 150.

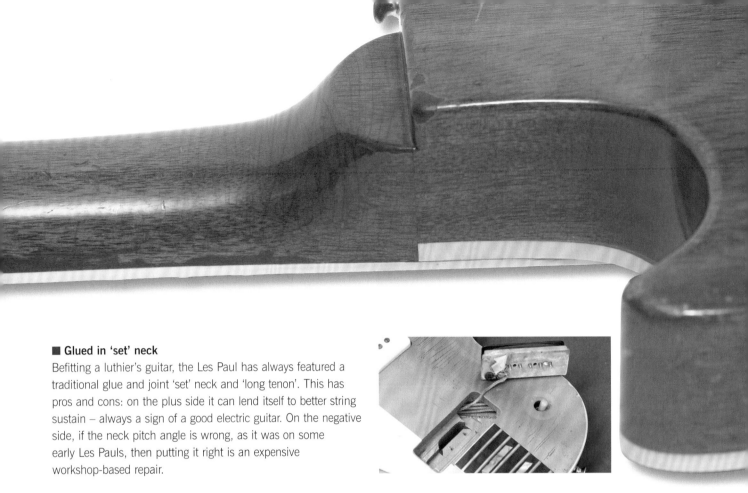

■ Glued in 'set' neck

Befitting a luthier's guitar, the Les Paul has always featured a traditional glue and joint 'set' neck and 'long tenon'. This has pros and cons: on the plus side it can lend itself to better string sustain – always a sign of a good electric guitar. On the negative side, if the neck pitch angle is wrong, as it was on some early Les Pauls, then putting it right is an expensive workshop-based repair.

■ Four control knobs

Each of the two pickups on the early Les Pauls has a designated tone and volume control enabling pre-set tones for lead and rhythm playing. Again this arrangement was adapted, in this case from the CES archtop guitars of 1951. The knobs themselves are of a distinctive early 1950s shape, and were manufactured from tenite butyrate plastic, made by 'local' firm Hughes Tools and Mfg Co, Michigan.

stems from the style '0' of 1903. The Gibson logo was originally the 'joined-up dot' type but soon changed to the 'separate dot' version, though the actual font remains virtually the same. The headstock pitch is 17°.

The tuners were originally Klusons and the fancy pegs are known to collectors as 'tulips'.

■ The three-way switch pickup selector

This was originally unlabelled, but by 1953 a cream plastic surround ferrule carried the options of 'lead & rhythm' – here extremely faded. This labelling epitomised the prevailing assumption in these early days of electric guitar: 'bridge p.u.' for solos 'neck p.u.' for rhythm. The switch naturally offered the 'in the middle' combined pickups option.

■ Conventional three-a-side tuner array and headstock

The Les Paul has always featured Gibson's traditional headstock. The size and shape has varied in detail but the basic layout

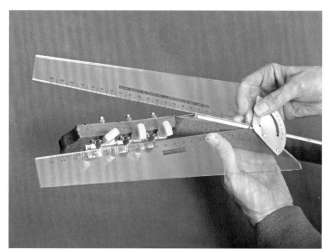

Know your classic Les Paul 'Standard'

The Les Paul 'Standards' of 1958–60 are the Holy Grail of the electric guitar world. Roughly 1,700 were made, and officially only those from 1960 are actually designated 'Standard'.

Guitars produced prior to 1960 are simply Les Paul 'Regular' models with humbuckers and, usually, a sunburst finish.

LEFT Quilt Top '59

RIGHT '60 Standard

■ 'Florentine' cutaway

By the standards of the late 1950s this gave generous access to the higher frets. The 'Regular' and 'Standard' have 22 frets, giving the player top D the minor 7th in the guitar's home key of E. The fret gauge is in the range 2.4mm–2.68mm.

■ Strap button

Located on the top bout – the Les Paul is designed to be played standing up; boots on the front stage monitor optional.

Given the desirability and rarity of the originals, Gibson have tried many times to come up with a 'new' option that fits the bill for a practical working guitar.

Presently the guitar is available in several different guises which reflect the subtle changes that occurred over the years 1958–60. There are discrete Gibson '58, '59 and '60 models in their Custom Shop range, as well as a Les Paul Classic in their regular output and several Epiphone versions for the budget market. Our overview will focus on the key generic features of the 'Standard' and also indicate some of the details that have changed.

■ Richly figured maple

One of critical factors in a collector's valuation of a 'Standard' is the quality and intensity of the figured grain in the matched maple top.

■ Tune-O-Matic bridge and stop tail

By 1957 the Les Paul had evolved a stable bridge arrangement with adequate scope for adjustment.

■ Humbucking pickups

Though not the first Gibson guitar to have Seth Lover's revolutionary humbuckers, the Les Paul is the guitar that has most come to define their classic sound.

■ **24¾in-scale fully bound mahogany neck**
With rosewood fingerboard and trapezoid position markers.

■ **Fingerboard with a Gibson traditional fairly flat radius of 12in**
The flatter radius of the 'Standard' was ironically unfashionable by 1958 but found its fans as the blues boom guitarists of the late '60s discovered that this flatter profile lends itself to choke-free string 'bends'.

■ **Gibson headstock**
The smaller-type traditional headstock features the 'separate dot' Gibson logo and a shield-type cover to the truss rod access.

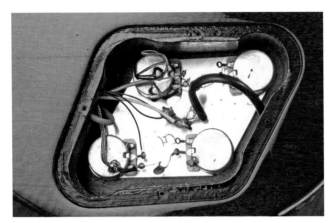

■ Easy access electrics

A touch of genius here, as all the electrical controls can be accessed by removing a few Phillips screws – there's no need to de-string or remove a mass of screws for an emergency repair. In researching his guitar Les Paul had availed himself of some earlier Epiphone archtops that featured a rear trapdoor for electrical access, but this was a first on a professional-class *solid* guitar.

■ Paired volume and tone controls

These and associated capacitors are all easily replaced or cleaned.

■ Pickup selector

Robust and easily accessible, the switch needs a special tool for safe removal without scratching, but is otherwise a good, simple, performance-friendly design.

■ Jack output socket

Primitive, simple, effective, not particularly elegant – but it does the job.

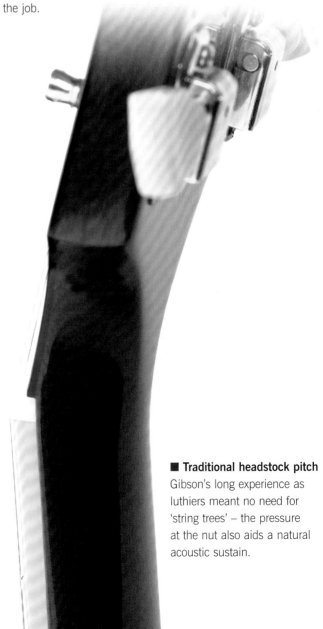

■ Traditional headstock pitch

Gibson's long experience as luthiers meant no need for 'string trees' – the pressure at the nut also aids a natural acoustic sustain.

■ **Enclosed machines**
Klusons were the natural
choice for early 'Standards'
and are now replaced on
current models by look-alikes
with better wind ratios and
better internal components.

■ **A separate removable pickguard**
A traditional approach as previously used on Gibson's archtops,
the guard floats off the guitar thereby not impeding sustain. It
is also removable if desired, for better appearance and a clearer
picking space. Many 'Standards' are now supplied without a
pickguard to better display the 'burst top.

■ **Clear picking space**
The 'Standard' always had two
pickups, each distinct in their
roles at picking up a different
sample of string harmonics.
This approach also leaves
a useful clear picking space
between pickups.

The illustrious 'House of Epiphone'

'Rivals and partners'

In the early 21st century it's easy to perceive Epiphone as merely Gibson's 'budget brand'. However, the Epiphone marque, established in 1873, has in fact a long and distinguished history of its own, 21 years longer than that of Gibson!

The Epiphone story begins in Sparta, Greece, in 1863 with the birth of Anastasios Stathopoulos, son of Nicolas, a timber merchant. In family mythology a precocious Anastasios was just ten years old when he built his first instruments, including Greek lutes and some violins. In 1877 the family moved to Smyrna in Asiatic Turkey.

Epimanondas (Epi) was born in 1893 to Anastasios's wife Marianthe, and it is this son who would give Epiphone its name. The original Epimanondas was an Ancient Greek military hero.

By this time Anastasios has established a large instrument factory in Smyrna making violins, mandolins, lutes and traditional Greek lioutos.

In 1903, following ethnic persecution by the Turks, Anastasios moved his family to the New World, specifically New York City. When Anastasios died in 1915 Epi was left in charge, and the modern Epiphone company began when, in 1923, he combined his name with the Greek word *phone* ('sound') and established Epiphone as a banjo brand name. In 1928 Epiphone introduced a line of guitars, most of them with carved tops in the Gibson style.

Throughout the 1930s Epiphone Inc became one of the USA's main guitar companies, and engaged with its chief rival Gibson in competitive battles of one-upmanship – who could build the biggest and loudest 'orchestral' guitars? Could anyone compete with Epiphone's 1935 super-wide 'Emperor' guitar? Epiphone were also innovators, introducing an adjustable-polepiece electric pickup as early as 1937.

The most famous early Epiphone jazz players were Tony Mottola, Allan Reuss and Dick McDonough with Benny Goodman, and Jack Teagarden and the illustrious George Van Eps with Ray Noble.

Epiphone became an important part of the Les Paul story in 1941, as Les Paul started to build his experimental 'Log' guitars in 'downtime' at the Epiphone factory on 14th Street, New York. These guitars consisted of a 4in by 4in timber core with Epiphone body halves crudely attached to maintain the appearance of a conventional archtop guitar – a sort of prototype ES 335. For more on these experiments *see page 8*. Lester continues to admire and endorse Epiphone guitars, with a 1930s 'De Luxe' a prized piece in his personal collection alongside Eddie Lang's L5 and one of Django Reinhardt's Maccaferris.

Sadly in 1943 Epi Stathopoulo died of leukaemia and the company suffered a lot of internal management problems. It fell on hard times during the post-war years, and by the mid-'50s was making few instruments, mostly upright basses and a series of Harry Volpe student-model guitars.

In 1957 Gibson's parent company, Chicago Musical Instruments (CMI), bought Epiphone for $20,000. The object was principally to acquire Epiphone's upright bass production equipment, but CMI decided to make Epiphone a division of Gibson and revived the Epiphone name. A set of new acoustics and electrics was unveiled in 1958 and in 1960 Epiphone production moved to Gibson's site in Kalamazoo, Michigan.

By 1961 Epiphone had a firm hold in Nashville, where Ernest Tubb presented his entire 'Texas Troubadours' with Epis. Marshall Grant also played his upright Epi bass in Johnny Cash's band, and Grady Martin played his Broadway on countless Nashville sessions.

Epi endorser Al Caiola was awarded his own model guitar in 1963 and played it on hit records including the themes from *Bonanza* and *The Magnificent Seven*.

A huge breakthrough came in 1964. Ironically, in England the Epiphone brand was perceived as 'Gibson' *but superior* – the argument being that they were the same guitars but made in smaller numbers with better quality control! This was certainly the perception in my home town of Liverpool, and as soon as they could afford a second guitar The Beatles' George Harrison, John Lennon and Paul McCartney each bought an Epiphone Casino, a guitar similar to Gibson's ES 330. Paul used his for the guitar solos on *Ticket To Ride*. George used his Casino – which, like his Gretsch, was equipped with a Bigsby vibrato – to play the scale passages in *Hello Goodbye*. All three

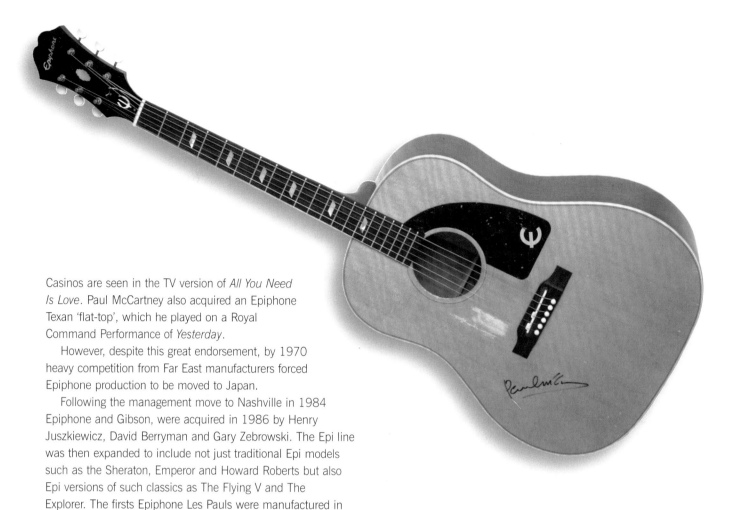

Casinos are seen in the TV version of *All You Need Is Love*. Paul McCartney also acquired an Epiphone Texan 'flat-top', which he played on a Royal Command Performance of *Yesterday*.

However, despite this great endorsement, by 1970 heavy competition from Far East manufacturers forced Epiphone production to be moved to Japan.

Following the management move to Nashville in 1984 Epiphone and Gibson, were acquired in 1986 by Henry Juszkiewicz, David Berryman and Gary Zebrowski. The Epi line was then expanded to include not just traditional Epi models such as the Sheraton, Emperor and Howard Roberts but also Epi versions of such classics as The Flying V and The Explorer. The firsts Epiphone Les Pauls were manufactured in Korea in 1989.

In 1993, under the leadership of Jim 'Epi' Rosenberg, the Epiphone line was further expanded to offer every style of guitar to the player on a budget. But at the same time Epiphone's historic reputation is maintained by the 'Nashville USA Collection' – limited edition models that are the first American-made Epiphones in over 20 years. Gibson's Montana division followed in 1994 with limited editions of the Epiphone flat top models Excellente, Frontier and Texan. In 2008 Epiphone introduced a Slash 'Signature' Les Paul.

My thanks to Epiphone Mfg Co for much of the above information.

❝ If I had to choose one electric guitar it would be this. ❞

Paul McCartney

Setting up and tuning

Achieving the perfect 'action' for your style of playing. In my experience a well set up budget Epiphone is a far more useful guitar than a poorly aligned 1960 Gibson 'Standard'. Most importantly it is almost impossible to tune a poorly set up instrument.

LEFT Using a Tune-O-Medic lever for raising a Tune-O-Matic.

RIGHT Gibson Custom Shop Quilt Top.

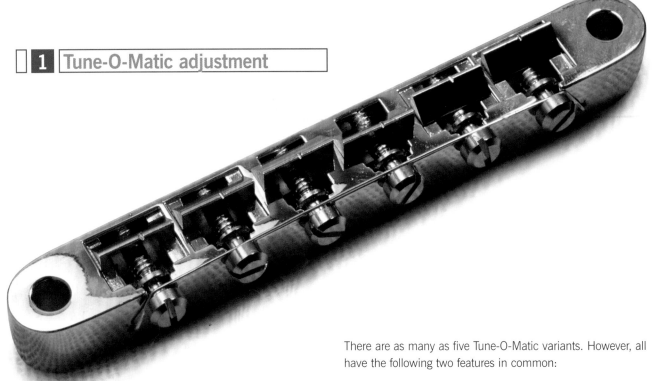

1 Tune-O-Matic adjustment

There are as many as five Tune-O-Matic variants. However, all have the following two features in common:

■ Saddles individually adjustable for string length.

■ Thumbwheel adjustment at both ends of the bridge for string height.

Tech Tip

Adjusting a Tune-O-Matic 'down' whilst maintaining string tension is usually not a problem. However, adjusting it 'up' without strain or damage to the guitar finish is easiest using a specialist tool. The old hands at Gibson Kalamazoo invented a makeshift jack for this. These days you can get a Tune-O-Medic from Stewart MacDonald. This simple but very strong lever has a protective felt back to preserve your guitar's lacquer.

Frank Marvel

The differences include:

■ Steel and brass-plated saddles (1952 onwards), bone saddles (1960) and white nylon saddles (1961). From 1961 metal saddles return.

■ A top screw arrangement for height adjustment – Epiphone only on current models.

■ A spring wire retainer (1962 onwards) for the saddles. This is not found on the original ABR-1 but is found on most new guitars, including Epiphones. For the sake of authenticity it is missing on many Custom Shop and vintage look-alikes.

■ The 'Nashville' version of the Tune-O-Matic has more scope for string length adjustment. This reflects the modern tendency towards lighter gauge strings, which often require more 'travel' on the bass strings to achieve a perfect octave at the 12th fret.

■ The 'Robot' Tune-O-Matic has onboard electronics for automatic intonation detection and communication with the servo machine heads.

■ Sometimes the Tune-O-Matic sits on a visible bridge post

set into the body of the guitar. At other times, as with this 'Custom', the bridge posts are countersunk.

■ Some recent Gibson Tune-O-Matics have individual spring saddle retainers.

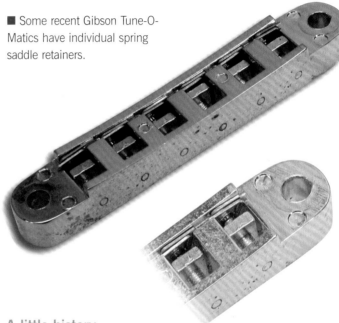

A little history

The Les Paul first appeared in 1952 with a rather precarious trapeze bridge/tailpiece – which didn't really work. By 1953 (see case study '53 Goldtop) this had been replaced by a wrap-over bridge/tailpiece combo. However, early adopter Muddy Waters had guitarist Pat Hare using Muddy's trapeze Goldtop in his band as late as 1960.

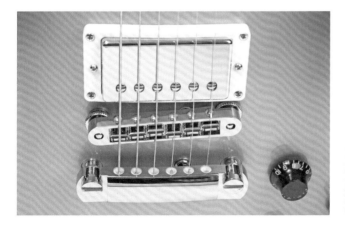

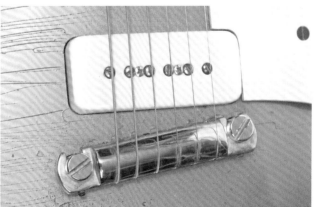

Setting the string height

Seeking better intonation adjustment, in 1956 Gibson introduced the Tune-O-Matic bridge, designed by a team headed by Ted McCarty. This offered *overall* height adjustment effected by two thumb-screws, and fine *length* adjustment for each individual string effected by a straight fine-thread screw arranged through the individual string saddles.

More recent budget-line Epiphone Tune-O-Matics have a 'top screw' arrangement which makes height adjustment easier.

■ Action

When guitarists refer to 'a good action' on their guitars they are actually referring to a complex interplay of factors:

■ The nut – its overall height and the depth of individual string grooves within the nut are immensely critical.
■ Neck relief – contrary to common belief, when under string tension the neck should be slightly convex, allowing the strings sufficient room for their complex excursion.
■ Fret wear – properly aligned frets are essential and these must be free of the groove wear that's a natural result of regular playing or, sometimes, excessively hard string materials.
■ The fretboard radius should be mirrored at the bridge – on a Les Paul this may mean some subtle filing of individual saddles, as individual height adjustment is not 'customer' adjustable. See check of 12in radius at bridge below.

■ Is the neck tilt correct? If not this is an expensive and luthier-only repair – one of the 'cons' of a traditional sustain-enhancing glued-in neck.
■ Are the string gauges appropriate to the guitar and its player's picking style?
■ Are the strings a matched set? Mixing gauges is a sophisticated art which requires a complementary set-up.

✎ Tech Tip

Beware stainless steel strings – great sound, but harder than your frets, which can mean a premature and expensive fret job.

John Diggins – Luthier

■ So why might you wish to adjust the overall string height?

Perhaps you are experimenting with different string gauges to achieve a different sound or style of playing – heavy gauge strings ideal for bottleneck slide guitar or super slinky 009s for three-semitone string bends? These extremes will require significant bridge adjustment.

String heights and all their parameters eventually come down to the preferences and styles of individual players. However, here are the Gibson recommended working references for an average Les Paul set-up:

Neck radius	String height at the 12th fret	
12in	Bass side	Treble side
	5/64in	3/64in

■ The nut

Before blaming the bridge for a 'too high' action it's worth checking the nut. This inauspicious bit of bone or plastic contributes hugely to the tone action and 'feel' of a guitar. The nut and its individual slots must be high enough to allow the strings free excursion but low enough and with slots cut smoothly and of appropriate size to accommodate the string gauges in use. A good guide for a Les Paul fitted with 'tens' (010-042) is .008in at the first fret first string.

1 Check the current action height at the 12th fret with a regular car feeler gauge. This will probably entail the combining of several individual gauges to make up Gibson's guideline recommendation of 3/64in on the treble side.

An alternative approach would be to use a metalworkers' steel rule with the required 1/32 and 1/64 increments (or decimal equivalent). The critical measurement is the distance from the top of the fret to the bottom of the string.

2 If the action measures too high on the treble side then turning the Tune-O-Matic thumbscrew clockwise will lower the action.

Do this slowly, checking all the time for any severe 'fret buzz' resulting from going too low, until the desired compromise is reached. Bear in mind that the simple two-point engineering involved will mean that to some extent *all* the strings will be lowered.

The same operation can be achieved on some Tune-O-Matics with a 5.5mm flathead screwdriver in the top slot – this adjustment option is most commonly found on Epiphone guitars. Again a clockwise micro-turn takes the bridge down (shown for bass strings). NB: The bridge responds quickly, so make any turns in small increments.

3 Make a similar measurement and adjustment to the bass side of the bridge and recheck any effects on the treble. Obviously a 'too low' bridge can equally be corrected by an anticlockwise adjustment of the thumbscrews.

Raising a Tune-O-Matic is sometimes difficult, as you are working against the downward pressure of the strings. The answer is to use a Tune-O-Medic bridge jack – not forcing the thumbscrews with a pair of finish-endangering pliers!

Often the crude two-point adjustment can still leave some individual strings too high or too low. This is best checked with a radius gauge.

4 If an individual saddle is too high then carefully and slowly filing the slot with a gauged nut file will do the trick – always checking constantly with the radius gauge. NB: Always file to leave the fulcrum edge at the 'neck' side of the saddle, at the same time avoiding filing the 'body' of the bridge!

5 If an individual saddle is too low then the choice is between lowering all the others to match, and then raising the whole bridge, or fitting a new individual saddle. This choice must obviously be made on the basis of the severity of the specific misalignment. The saddles are available 'un-notched' from the usual outlets (see *Useful contacts* appendix).

Bear in mind that lowering or raising the bridge will necessarily affect the effective sounding length of the string, and this will inevitably require adjustment of the Tune-O-Matic's individual saddle screws to achieve a precise octave at the 12th fret – see further on in this chapter.

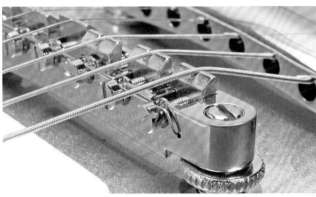

Setting the working string lengths

The Tune-O-Matic enables precise setting of the individual string lengths to achieve a perfect octave at the 12th fret.

■ So why would you need to do this?

If you change the Tune-O-Matic height, the gauge of your strings or adjust the truss rod it is likely that the precise individual string lengths will have also changed. The result is that when fretted your guitar sounds out of tune even when the open strings seem precisely 'in tune'.

■ A little background

There are two basic ways of changing the pitch of a vibrating guitar string – you can increase or decrease the string tension by adjusting the machine heads, as in normal tuning, or you can alter the string length by normal fretting on the fingerboard.

The frets on the fingerboard are arranged in a mathematical series of ascending decreasing intervals. The frets get closer together as we ascend to 'the dusty end of the fingerboard'. We won't get bogged down in the maths here.

The assumption of the correct function of the carefully worked-out fret intervals is that the string itself has a defined length. If all your guitar's strings were the same gauge or thickness we could dispense with Ted McCarty's bridge and simply have a straight-line arrangement of the bridge saddles.

In the real world your first string could be .010 gauge and your sixth string .050. The four other strings are usually gauged somewhere between these two. Fretting a string changes its tension slightly. A difference in string diameter affects the amount of change in string tension as it is fretted. This means that to sound 'in tune' the 1st string benefits from having a shorter effective length than the 2nd string and so on. Hence Ted's Tune-O-Matic.

I recommend you find a gauge of string that works for you, set the guitar up, and stick with that gauge.

■ Intonation

Note that raising or lowering the Tune-O-Matic will effectively alter the strings' sounding length and therefore the fine setting of the intonation should be attempted only *after* a comfortable bridge height has been established *(see page 39)*.

(see page 39)

1 Tune the open first string to E concert 440Hz. Check the 12th fret stopped note – is it the same? An electronic guitar tuner is a useful aid to a precise scientific assessment.

This will display any discrepancy in cents either sharp or flat. Both these notes and the 'octave' (12th fret) harmonic should be the same.

Tune-O-Matics can be fitted with screw heads facing the tailpiece *or* facing the pickups (the original arrangement); the guidance offered here refers to the latter. If your guitar has the former arrangement then the clockwise/anticlockwise instructions will necessarily reverse!

Note that a little masking tape or a well-placed duster on the pickup cover or stop bar will avoid accidental scratches being caused by the screwdriver.

2 If the string sound indicates flat at the 12th fret when compared to the 12th harmonic turn the saddle length adjustment screw clockwise, thereby moving the saddle towards the neck (shortening the effective sounding length).

If the note at the 12th fret sounds sharp when compared to the harmonic then the sounding length is too short and the saddle screw should be adjusted anticlockwise.

Tools required

■ **Flat-head screwdriver with 5mm blade.**
■ **Electronic tuner and guitar lead.**
■ **Duster.**
■ **Masking tape.**

Adjust the harmonic, 12th fret and open string until they all indicate the same note.

Repeat the process for all six strings.

Sometimes when you run out of 'travel' and the note is still flat or sharp at the 12th fret, the Tune-O-Matic saddles have to be reversed. This is a simple enough procedure, only occasionally made difficult by the saddle retaining spring. This can be awkward to remove – a little persuasion with some fine-nosed pliers and a suitably taped-up screwdriver usually does the trick, but *go gently* as you need the spring to retain its shape in order to remain effective when reinstalled.

Sometimes on reversal the saddle notch will need re-filing, ensuring the fulcrum edge is at the pickup side of the saddle.

Replacing the spring is another 'go gently' operation using suitably protected fine-nose pliers.

▌ Tech Tip

It's worth checking the intonation at the 19th fret of the first string (B natural) against the open B string. If the open B and E are in tune then the 19th fret and open B should not 'beat'. This applies equally to the 20th fret on the B string and the open G string. Similar checks should be tried on the 19th fret for all other strings.

John Diggins – Luthier

Designed by Paul Adelburt Bigsby (1899–1968), and currently made in Savannah, Georgia, USA (as well as being licensed for Far Eastern copies), the Bigsby guitar vibrato arm is probably the second most famous vibrato after Leo Fender's 'synchronised floating trem'.

In the late 1940s Paul Bigsby, Les Paul and Leo Fender were all friends and together they kicked around ideas for a solid-bodied guitar with the then fashionable vibrato-glissandi and rich sustain qualities of an 'Hawaiian' steel guitar. They all came up with slightly different solutions to this challenge and Paul Bigsby was certainly in the vibrato arm business before Leo (probably as early as 1948, while Leo's appeared in 1954).

In truth the Bigsby arm is not as innovative as Leo's and is both very heavy and perhaps a little more clumsy in operation. However, it does have its own distinctive character of vibrato, heard to great effect on the recordings of Duane Eddy, Chet Atkins and many Rockabilly guitarists.

Strangely the Bigsby is most associated with hollow body Gretsch and Gibson models, *not* solid body guitars. However, the Les Paul guitar became available with a Bigsby to special order from the early 1950s and several high-profile guitarists – including Les Paul, Mick Taylor and Keith Richards – have used Bigsby appointed Les Pauls.

Practicalities and intonation issues

Perhaps the first thing to consider with a Bigsby is weight! Our 'Black Beauties' weigh 9½lb (4.3kg) without a trem and 10½lb (4.8kg) with. This is an aluminium trem with gold plating – the B7G model, with black infilling on the Bigsby logo and a gap in the heel plate for a strap fixing.

Although the Bigsby is less subtle and responsive than Leo Fender's or any of the other 'synchronised' trems, there *are* plus factors with Paul Bigsby's design:

■ The extra weight behind the Tune-O-Matic does give more rigidity and 'tone' to the guitar's acoustic and amplified sound, perhaps lowering the guitar's principal resonant frequency – often a beneficial effect.

■ Unlike a 'floating' trem, the single powerful 'motorcycle compression' spring of the Bigsby causes much less pitch discrepancy when physically bending strings, *ie* you can manually pitch bend strings 1, 2 and 3 whilst sustaining a pedal bass note and the latter remains *relatively* stable. Try this on a floating Strat trem and you may unintentionally enter the world of bitonality!

■ By the same token a broken string on a correctly set up Bigsby will leave the rest of the guitar fairly in tune. On a floating trem you enter the world of atonality.

However, keeping a Bigsby working well and even replacing strings does set certain unique challenges.

The first thing to know is that there are at least 12 different variants of the Bigsby vibrato, some cosmetic but many critical to its effective use. If you have a Les Paul with a factory-fitted Bigsby it will be the correct type. However, retro-fitted Bigsbys need to be carefully selected and Bigsby currently offer aluminium and 'gold'-plated types specifically with the Les Paul in mind. These are the B7, B70 and B12, all offered in plain aluminium or 'gold' plated.

Maintenance

■ Lubricate the spring extremely sparingly – over-lubrication may cause damage to the all-important 'cushion' washer.

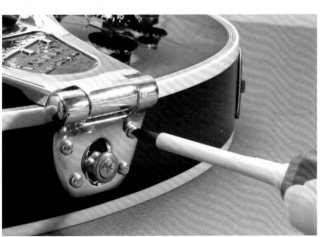

■ Lubricate the whole string path – the nut with graphite, saddles with a microscopic amount of '3 in 1' oil and the Bigsby roller with a little Vaseline or ChapStick. Be especially careful not to stain any 'gold'-plated fittings where present.

■ Replacement springs, fibre washers and bearings are readily available from Bigsby, and a 50-year-old trem may often benefit from replacement of these heavily mechanical parts – any wear-induced discrepancies will naturally affect the precarious stability of the mechanism.

■ For tuning stability it is essential to ensure that all the fitting screws are tight. This requires a '2' point Phillips for the top fixings and a '1' point Phillips for the end plate.

Stringing a Bigsby-fitted Les Paul

1 Crimp the new string into a curve at the ball end – an awkward job!

2 Feed the string underneath, around and over the axle.

3 Place the ball end of the string onto the axle pin.

4 Keep the tension on the string with a capo at the 7th fret holding the ball in place on the axle.

5 You could alternatively try pushing a wedge of foam rubber into the space under the axle to keep the string in place on the pin during winding.

6 Wind the string onto the tuning machine, tune to pitch, remove the capo and/or the foam wedge.

In the 1940s Les Paul loved to experiment with his guitars and was amongst the first to try combinations of two and more pickups. His own Les Paul guitars are Heath Robinson works of genius with phase switches, remote controls and all possible pickup configurations.

Most performing guitarists prefer simplicity in their stage instrument and the standard Les Paul switch on a two-pickup guitar offers the expected neck/both/bridge arrangement. The 'Custom' three-pickup guitar offers bridge, bridge and middle, and neck alone. Peter Frampton has a more complex arrangement on his signature guitar (see case study, page 142).

Replacing a three-way selector

Bear in mind that three-way switches on Gibson and Epiphone models differ in quality and in thread sizes. For instance, if you wish to replace the plastic knob on the American guitars the thread is 32G 5/32in, available from Switchcraft, and on Epiphones 40G 1/8in.

The Epiphone 'Standard' we are using for our modifications and repairs comes from China with a short, and often short-lived, three-way switch that is well worth replacing.
The longer-barrelled professional-type switch usually found on Gibson Les Pauls is readily available and less prone to intermittence and 'crackle and pop'. It will fit in the cavity on most Epiphones.

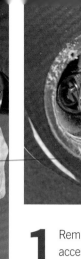

2 Remove the knurled retaining ring using the designed tool or a pair of pliers suitably 'softened' (try some masking tape on the jaws).

3 Unsolder the old switch (labelling the wires if you're in any doubt as to their orientation). If, like me, you are a less than professional electrician then protect the guitar from solder with a suitably placed cloth.

4 Unscrew the knurled ring from the new switch.

5 Position the new switch and resolder.

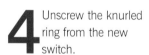

6 Orientate the new switch so that it functions as per the rhythm/lead labelling. The 'aged' switch knob is a nice touch.

1 Remove the switch rear access hatch with a 1-point Phillips.

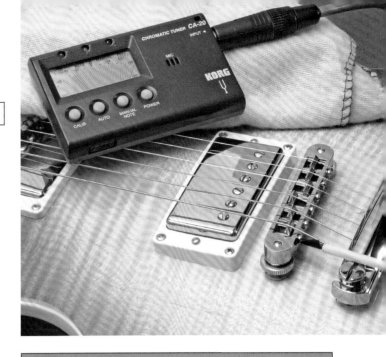

4 | Tuning

A properly set up Les Paul will tune up and stay in tune even when the player employs an excess of Spinal Tap abuse.

When the Les Paul first appeared the only reference options available for accurate tuning were tuning forks, as used by violinists and piano tuners, and 'pitch pipes', a device similar to a mouth-organ with six 'open string' reference pitches. Pianos when available were often pitched fractionally 'flat' due to neglect.

The introduction of electronic tuners since the early 1980s has offered guitarists an increasingly accurate reference tool. The key word here is 'reference'. The open strings of a guitar tuned to correspond with an accurate electronic tuner provide a great starting point for accurate tuning. However, it is essential to remember that the guitar, like the piano, is a 'tempered' instrument. Even the most accurately fretted and set up Les Paul is built on a tempered tuning system that compromises the science of pitch by considering 'enharmonic' notes such as C# and Db as the same note, which they are not!

■ Tempered tuning

If we all played fretless guitars this would not be an issue. However, there are very few fretless Les Pauls and even less fretless guitarists.

■ Tempered tuning in practice

In the real world a tuning compromise has been reached, referred to as 'equal temperament', and most rock and pop musicians will happily accept the faint 'out of tuneness' associated with certain chords in certain keys and positions on the fingerboard.

In fact in single-string solo playing many players consciously or unconsciously 'temper' certain notes slightly sharp or flat by a combination of listening and microtonally 'bending' notes as they play. This technique, combined with pitch-dependent vibrato, is so indigenous to the guitar as to be second nature. This factor even contributes to the guitar's expressive 'human' quality – keyboards, for instance, can never really do this.

For accurate rhythm playing which naturally incorporates chords many guitarists will 'tune to key', using an electronic tuner for reference and then 'tempering' the relevant notes within the pivotal chords of a song to reach an acceptable compromise that 'sounds' musical.

■ The bottom line

Tune your Les Paul to EADGBE (or whatever exotic tuning you favour) using a tuner for reference, then 'temper' as required.

Under the recording microscope

In the 1980s and '90s I worked as an independent record producer. In that role I encountered many young bands during their first serious recording sessions. Most had never had their guitars set up properly and virtually all were unaware of the wider scope of guitar tuning beyond tuning the open strings via an electronic tuner. Consequently, many a frustrating hour of valuable session time was spent adjusting string lengths and tempering guitar tunings to the key of the song to be recorded. It's always worth checking your set-up before an important recording session.

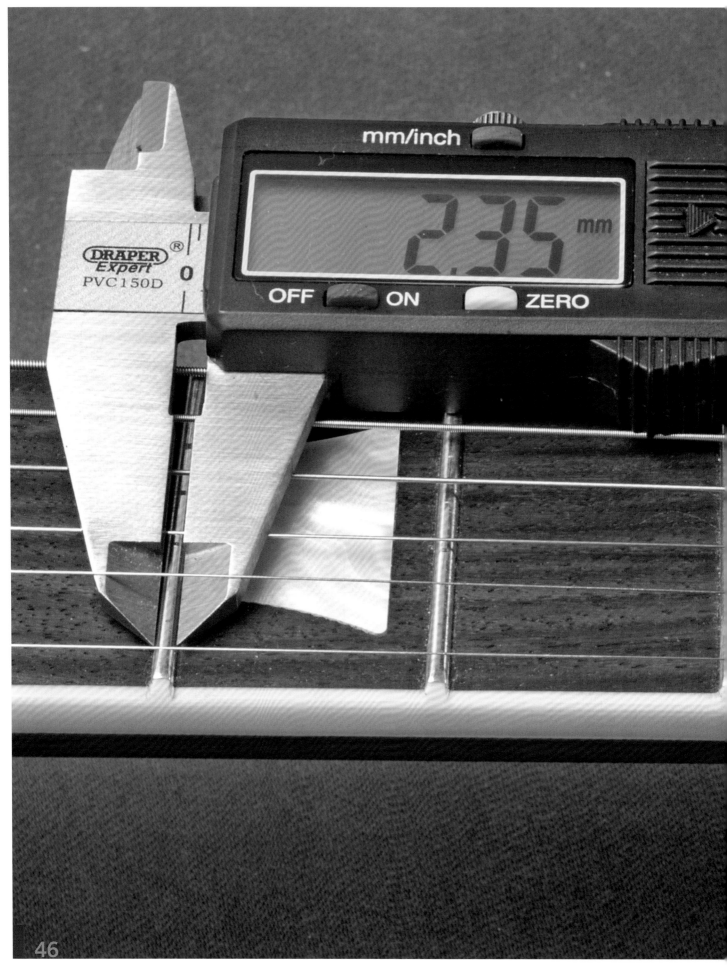

Repairs, maintenance and adjustments

The regular Les Paul guitar is a fascinating piece of 1950s technology which requires little maintenance and lubrication. Many tasks are guitarist-friendly but you may need a few specialist luthiers' tools. Beware of skilled areas such as sunburst lacquer re-touching unless you have the necessary skills and equipment.

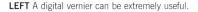

LEFT A digital vernier can be extremely useful.

RIGHT Gibson Custom 2 p.u.

Safety first

Generally speaking the electric guitar is no more dangerous to play or work on than its acoustic cousin. However, there are inevitably some additional hazards of which you should be aware.

Electric shock

Sadly many guitar players have either been killed or badly burned through accidental exposure to mains current. Though the UK's adoption of 240V may seem to present a greater risk than the USA's 110V, it's actually the amps that are the killer not the volts! Amperes are the measure of current, and high currents are the ones to avoid.

Guitar amplifiers run happily on domestic supplies at relatively low current ratings, so the situation of one guitarist one amp is a pretty safe scenario, especially if we observe a few precautions:

■ Always ensure a good earth or ground connection. This allows a safe path to earth for any stray current, which always flows along the easiest path. The earth or ground offers a quicker route to earth than through you and therein lies its safety potential.

■ Never replace fuses with the wrong value, *eg* a 5-amp fuse in a 3-amp socket. Fuses are there to protect us and our equipment from power surges. A higher value means less protection. Never replace a fuse with a bodge such as silver foil or similar. This offers no protection at all.

■ Consider using an earth leakage trip or similar circuit-breaker in any situation where you have no control or knowledge of the mains power.

■ Maintain your mains leads. Check them regularly for damage and strained wires. The earth wire must be in place.

■ Never operate an amplifier with the safety cover removed, especially valve amplifiers known for their HT circuits.

■ Never put drinks on or near amplifiers.

■ Never touch a stage lighting circuit or lamp. Apart from mains electricity issues they are often also dangerously hot. Leave stage lamps to qualified electricians.

Beware of

■ Multi amp/multi PA scenarios that aren't professionally administered. Professional PA and lighting supervisors are very safety-conscious and trained in health and safety to a legal minimum requirement. The danger comes with 'semi pro' and amateur rigs which aren't closely scrutinised. If you're in any doubt don't plug in until you've talked to the on-site supervisor and feel you can trust his assurances.

■ Unknown stage situations, especially those which feature big lighting rigs. This is easily said but hard to adhere to. Even the most modest gigs nowadays have quite sophisticated lights and sound. The crucial issue is that all the audio equipment is connected to the same PHASE. Danger particularly arises when microphones are connected to one PHASE and guitars to another. A guitar/vocalist could find himself as the 'bridge' between 30 amps of current! If in any doubt be rude and ask.

Repetitive strain injury

Guitarists need to think about posture, warm-up routines and avoiding over-practicing. RSI is not funny and affects millions of guitarists. Generate good habits early and stick to them.

Hearing damage

Leo Fender's first guitar amp, the K&F of 1945, knocked out a feverish 4W of audio. In fact they were so mild mannered that some of them lacked so much as a volume control. Gibson amps were very similar

The first Fender Bassman amps boasted 26W and by 1964 The Beatles had the first 100W VOX amps, specifically made to cope with concerts in vast football stadiums and the noise of immense screaming crowds.

By 1970 100W was the norm for a guitar 'head' in a small club and the first 10,000W PA systems had rocked Woodstock.

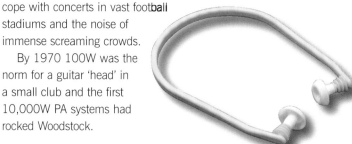

Pete Townshend of The Who first complained of the hearing impairment tinnitus in the mid '70s and for many years refused to tour with a band as his hearing worsened.

The key to saving your hearing is 'dose' figures. Research has shown that you risk damage if exposed to sound 'dose' levels of 90dB or above for extended periods. Health and safety limits for recording studios now recommend no more than 90dBA ('A' standing for average) per eight-hour day, these levels to be reduced dramatically if the period is longer or the dBA higher.

Transient peaks, as in those produced by a loud snare drum or hi-hat, can easily push levels beyond these figures. Be careful where you stand in relation to drums and amplifiers – a small movement can effect a dramatic change in transient sound level. Don't be afraid to ask about peak and average levels. Your ears are your greatest asset as a musician, so don't be embarrassed into thinking you can't question sound levels.

Chemical Hazards

Paints and solvents
Traditionally the Les Paul is painted with nitrocellulose lacquer and this practice continues on many guitars, especially Vintage reissues. Nitrocellulose lacquers produce a very hard yet flexible, durable finish that can be polished to a high gloss. The drawbacks of these lacquers include the hazardous nature of the solvent, which is flammable, volatile and toxic. The dangers inherent in the inhalation of spray paints are serious enough to be covered by legal statutes in the USA, the UK, and Europe.

Symptoms
- Acute and chronic ingestion: Large doses may cause nausea, narcosis, weakness, drowsiness, and unconsciousness.
- Inhalation: Irritation to nose and throat. At high concentrations, same effects as ingestion.
- Skin: Cracking of skin, dermatitis, and secondary infections.
- Eyes: Irritation.
- Symptoms of overexposure: Repeated skin contact may cause dermatitis, while the skin defatting properties of this material may aggravate an existing dermatitis.
  (Source: Material Safety Data Sheet.)

Polyurethane
Vapours may accumulate in inadequately ventilated/confined areas. Vapours may form explosive mixtures with air. Vapours may travel long distances and flashback may occur. Closed containers may explode when exposed to extreme heat.

Symptoms
- Ingestion: May be similar to inhalation symptoms – drowsiness, dizziness, nausea, irritation of digestive tract, depression, aspiration hazard.
- Inhalation: Dizziness, drowsiness, fatigue, weakness, headache, unconsciousness.
- Skin: Drying, cracking, dermatitis.

- Eyes: Burning, tearing, reddening. Possible transient corneal injury or swelling of conjunctiva.
  (Source: Carbon Black Carcinogen by IARC, Symptoms of Overexposure.)

Recommended precautions
Always wear goggles/full face shield and other protective equipment. Avoid skin contact by wearing protective clothing. Take a shower and bathe your eyes after exposure. Wash contaminated clothing thoroughly before reusing it.

...So, with all this in mind, remember that the addresses of recommended guitar repair men and spray shops can be found in your local *Yellow Pages*.

If you really feel you want to customise your Les Paul body then you must take extreme precautions, particularly to avoid inhalation of the dangerous mist created by the spray process.

A passive mask available from DIY stores will only offer the most minimal protection. If in any doubt consult the paint manufacturer for detailed precautions specific to the paint type you've chosen.

Tools and working facilities

Many Les Paul adjustments can be done using regular domestic workshop tools. However, this guitar originated from a luthier tradition and certain specialist tools are occasionally required.

Necessary workshop tools

Many of the tools listed below can double up as your essential gig bag wrap, but as you don't have to carry all of them around we can be less concerned about weight and portability. Consequently it's very convenient, for instance, to have separate screwdrivers rather than the interchangeable-bit variety. Heftier wire cutters also make string changing a little easier.

■ Set of car feeler gauges (.002–.025) (0.05–1mm)
These are used for assessing and setting the string action height.

■ 12in (150mm) ruler with 1/32in and 1/64in increments (0.5mm increments)
Also used for setting and assessing the string action.

■ Light machine oil (3-in-1 or equivalent)
Can be used sparingly for lubricating the string path.

■ Set of Phillips-type screwdrivers, sizes '0', '1' and '2' point
It may seem a small point but we recommend using the correct size and type of screwdriver. Many valuable Les Pauls have survived 30 years on the road but often have a selection of odd screws and 'stripped' screw heads. These look unsightly, slow down maintenance and make the simplest job a chore. The correct 'point' size screwdriver will reduce screw stripping and is also less likely to skate across your prized paintwork.

Use type '0' point for some truss rod shields; type '1' point for pickguard, rear access covers, jack socket, machine head (Kluson type) and strap button; and type '2' point for some pickup height adjustments.

A screwdriver with interchangeable heads is an alternative option. However, you'll often need several heads at the same time, which means a lot of changing around. This option is nevertheless useful on the road, when a compact toolkit is more practical.

Sometimes an electric screwdriver can take the strain out of repetitive tasks, but be sure to protect the guitar as the screwdriver 'torques out'. *Never* use one on plastic parts, as old plastics become brittle and easily crack under sudden pressure.

■ **4mm straight-slot screwdriver**
For pickup height adjustment.

■ **Portable suction fixing vice**
This ingenious device is terrific if you have no suitable permanent workbench. Ideal for nut filing.

■ **Screw extractor HSS drills and tap wrenches**
For removing broken screws.

■ **Zap-It electric screwdriver attachment**
Makes light work of de-stringing guitars.

■ **Large 12mm/0.5in straight-slot screwdriver**
For the 'stop bar' type tailpiece. A specialist bridge/tailpiece tool is also available. (See *Useful contacts* appendix.)

■ **Electronic tuner**
An accurate electronic tuner with a jack socket as opposed to an internal microphone will make short work of adjusting the intonation of individual string lengths.

■ **Wire cutters**
For cutting strings to length. Overlong strings at the peghead are a safety hazard and tear up your gig bag.

■ **Peg winder**
Time saving, and avoids RSI when changing strings. Fit one to your electric screwdriver.

■ **Small penlight torch**
Useful for closer examination of details. Useful any time but especially in a stageside emergency.

■ **Tune-O-Medic kit**
For adjusting Tune-O-Matic bridges and stop bars. (See *Useful contacts* appendix.)

Henry Phillips

Have you wondered why Les Pauls feature Phillips-type screws? In the 1950s companies like Gibson were taking lessons from the streamlined assembly process at Henry Ford's car lines in Detroit. For these, Henry Phillips (1890–1958) had developed the cross-head screw. In 1936 The American Screw Co persuaded General Motors to use the Phillips-head screw in manufacturing Cadillacs, and by 1940 virtually every American automaker had switched to Phillips screws.

This new screw worked well with ratchet and electric screwdrivers, had greater torque, was self-centring and didn't slip from the slot so easily, avoiding damage to the valuable paintjob. The speed with which Phillips screws can be used was crucial to the auto assembly line. In addition, Phillips screws are almost impossible to over-screw, which was very important.

However, cam-out or torque-out makes tightly-driven Phillips screws fiendishly hard to remove and often damages the screw, the driver, and anything else a suddenly loose driver happens to hit. And whereas a coin or a piece of scrap metal can often be used to loosen a slot screw, nothing takes the place of a Phillips screwdriver. A flat-bladed driver or even a wrong-size Phillips just makes cam-out worse.

Beware: Phillips screwdrivers should not be used with Pozidrive screws (and vice versa). They are subtly different and when mixed they tend to ride out of the slot as well as rounding the corners of both the tool and the screw recess.

■ **Specialist wrench**
For pickup selector retaining screws. (See *Useful contacts* appendix.)

■ **Polish and cloth**
A soft duster for body and back of the neck, a lint-free cotton hankie for strings and fingerboard. Proprietary guitar polishes differ from household furniture polishes, which often contain silicone. The wax used in guitar polish is emulsified to avoid any sticky residue, especially under the heat from stage lighting.

■ **Tweezers**
For rescuing dropped screws from awkward cavities and removing hot wires during soldering.

Soldering tips

When soldering heat-sensitive parts such as pickups and potentiometers, it's quicker and safer to 'tin' all the components (this means applying a little solder) and then join them together for the minimum amount of time whilst applying heat from the iron.

■ Soldering iron

This should be at least 25W with a penlight tip. An iron is essential when replacing worn-out volume pots and three-way switches etc. It's worth investing in a stand with a sponge cleaner attached (Draper components 23554 or similar). A crocodile clip multi-arm is also useful for holding small components in place.

■ A tube of solder

Multicore-type non-acid resin.

■ Crocodile clips

Can be used as isolating 'heat sinks' – but not too close to the joins, as they'll hamper the operation by drawing away too much heat.

■ A solder syringe

Makes light work of drawing old solder from previous electrical joints.

✎ Tech Tip

The worst-case scenario with soldering is melting the plastic on interior wires – so be quick! But also keep the components steady: a wire moved during solder setting may cause a 'dry joint' and poor conductivity.

John Diggins – Luthier

Some vintage Gibsons still retain cloth-wire insulation, which doesn't melt but may start to disintegrate – I don't think anybody expected electric guitars to last 50 years!

Useful accessories

- Vaseline or ChapStick for lubrication.
- Silicone or graphite locksmiths' nut lubricant.
- Matchsticks or cocktail sticks for lubrication application and 'rawlplugging' loose screws.
- Pipe cleaners and cotton buds for cleaning awkward spots; an old electric toothbrush can also be useful.
- Radius gauges for setting the bridge saddles.
- An electronic multimeter for testing pickup circuits.
- A set of socket spanners are good for removing and tightening pot nuts, jack sockets and some modern machine heads.
- Mechanical and digital callipers – great for all sorts of detailed measurements.
- Loctite or similar multi-purpose glue.
- Craft knife for nut work.

- Thread gauges, useful for checking trem arm threads etc.
- Rubber hammer, safer in many situations on valuable instruments.
- Wire stripper.
- Lemon oil for rosewood fingerboards.
- Spare jack socket, 500K pot, knobs and pickup switch.
- Dental abrasives for fine-tuning a nut slot.

Working environment

Many guitar repairs and much maintenance can be safely carried out with the guitar resting in its hard shell case on a normal kitchen table or on a Workmate-type DIY bench, suitably padded. The photographs in this book are 80 per cent of work done at home on a Draper Workmate. However, *see page 49* for precautions regarding the inhalation of cellulose etc.

Outside the guitar case environment, a small 1m square of carpet sample bluetacked to a workbench can avoid a lot of inadvertent damage to guitar paintwork.

All the guitar techs and luthiers consulted for this book seemed to have their own ingenious home made tools for very specific jobs.

Essential gig bag accessories

Carrying a few spares can save you a long walk, but you have enough to carry to a gig without hauling your whole toolkit around. The mere essentials compactly rolled in a tool wrap will potentially save a lot of pre-gig hassle, and should fit in your gig bag or guitar case compartment.

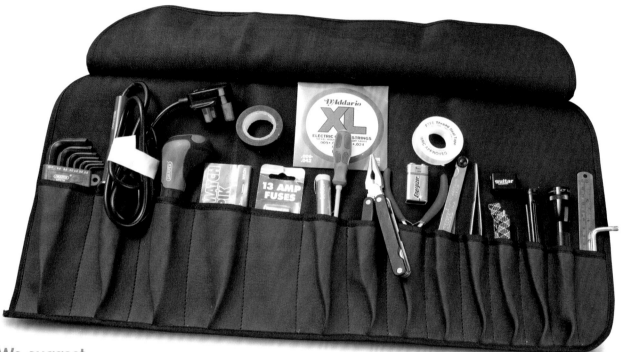

We suggest...

A multipoint screwdriver with Phillips or cross screw type '0', '1' and '2' point bits and small and medium point conventional straight heads. The Tune-O-Matic bridge utilises conventional 'straight ' slot screws as opposed to the Phillips variety found elsewhere on the guitar. A conventional screwdriver is useful to have around anyway for dealing with broken mains plugs and blown fuses.

- A small pair of wire snips for emergency string changes.
- Small 'emergency only' soldering iron and 6in of solder.
- Some 13-amp and 5-amp (UK) fuses as well as any specific to your area of touring (ie USA and European equivalents, etc).
- A PP3 battery (for FX).
- A penlight torch.
- Spare plectrums and/or finger picks.

- Allen/Hex keys for truss rod, etc.
- A nail file.
- A Leatherman or similar multitool
  – useful for a sharp blade and decent pliers.
- Capo.
- Insulating tape.
- Feeler gauges.
- 6in rule.
- An electronic tuner.
- Spare strings.
- Tune-O-Medic jack for **raising the Les Paul bridge.**
- Plumbers' PTFE tape – useful for securing loose control knobs.

Unfortunately, by having these with you you'll acquire a reputation as Mr Ever Ready, and before long everybody in the band will come to depend on your tools!

It's worth doing a little maintenance

…Or getting an expert to do it for you. The Les Paul is proving to be a classic survivor. Even the rigours of the world tour have been surmounted with the help of a good flight case and a little loving care. Clearly few of us would risk taking a '58–'60 'burst on the road, but barring abuse and given a few careful tweaks it would undoubtedly acquit itself well.

Vintage antiques

If you're lucky enough to own a vintage Les Paul then what you have in your possession is not just a good instrument but a piece of popular music history. Given its rarity, you must regard the guitar as you would any other valuable 'antique'.

Whilst such guitars are considered a valuable investment, I personally share the view of many antique furniture collectors that design and function are part of the charm of such items and therefore they are best kept in use. I hold no truck with the 'investor' who thinks a guitar is best consigned to a bank vault. For me this is missing the point, like the owner who never actually drives his Ferrari. If you check the world's museums you will see that unplayed instruments merely wilt and die.

So I recommend you enjoy your guitar whilst observing a few precautions:

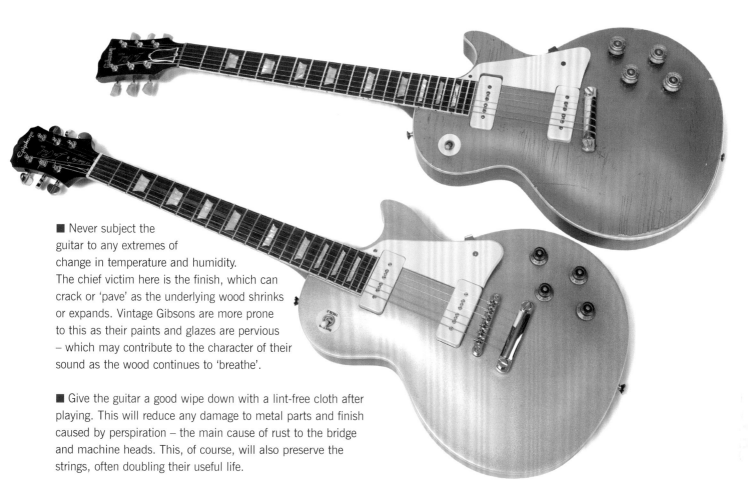

■ Never subject the
guitar to any extremes of
change in temperature and humidity.
The chief victim here is the finish, which can
crack or 'pave' as the underlying wood shrinks
or expands. Vintage Gibsons are more prone
to this as their paints and glazes are pervious
– which may contribute to the character of their
sound as the wood continues to 'breathe'.

■ Give the guitar a good wipe down with a lint-free cloth after
playing. This will reduce any damage to metal parts and finish
caused by perspiration – the main cause of rust to the bridge
and machine heads. This, of course, will also preserve the
strings, often doubling their useful life.

■ Keep moving parts suitably lubricated.

■ Use a good stable guitar stand. This sounds so obvious,
but many once fabulous instruments turn up on the repair
bench having been accidentally knocked off some precarious
perch. This particularly
applies to the Les Paul,
which has a vulnerable
weak point at the neck
head-stock joint. Combined
with the dense mass of
its body this guitar is an
accident waiting to happen.

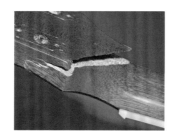

Authenticity

Many true 'relics' of the '50s have parts missing, particularly
knobs and switches. It is perfectly natural to want to replace
these. However, it is almost a custodial responsibility to replace
these tastefully. These guitars will outlive us and carry on being
worthwhile instruments for centuries. I predict the authentic
'early music' enthusiasts of 2050 will include people performing
Freddie King on authentic '50s Goldtops with 'tweed' Fender
amps. So seek out the most authentic replacement parts
possible. It's relatively easy to buy 'aged' plastic parts with a
suitable patina that ooze an atmosphere of smoky bars and long
years on the chitlin circuit (see *Useful contacts* appendix). Do,

however, make a careful note of any changes, as this will save
argument over authenticity at a later date.

Authenticity remains an issue 'under the hood', and with an
old instrument it is extremely prudent to conserve any original
cloth covered wiring and even use authentic '50s-type solders.
This may sound over the top at present but the collectors and
players of the next century will remember you warmly for taking
that extra bit of trouble.

■ Keep the original parts

Over the years I have personally accumulated a small collection
of bits from previous guitars, including a couple of bridge parts
from a '62 Fiesta Red Strat, my first proper guitar. Now in 1969
when I sold the guitar, these seemed to be scrap metal and
it never occurred to me to pass them on. But if the guitar still
exists, and it probably does (serial no 87827 – let me know if
you have it!), these old parts are an important piece of what
antiquarians call 'provenance'. A dealer may spot the 'new'
saddle pieces I obtained with great difficulty in
1966, and wonder if the guitar really is a '62
Fiesta Red, but if the present owner had **the**
old parts it completes a part of that story
which supports the authenticity of the
overall instrument. So put those old part**s**
in a safe place and label them with any
information you have.

An exception

John Diggins, the brilliant guitar maker behind the basses of Mark King and the guitars of Tony Iommi, does marvellous 'patch blends' on old finishes. I now think this approach is a good working compromise for newer instruments. A few years ago I presented him with a sunburst Fender Precision bass that some hooligan had sanded down to the wood but only on the front! I thought that only a complete respray would provide a pleasing finish but John immediately recommended a 'patch'. I was sceptical but on seeing the results I was stunned, the guitar looks wonderful and is still 50 per cent original finish; the odd 'ding' on the original finish gives the guitar a bit of history, but it no longer looks like an industrial accident, which it did before. As a mark of John's true craftsmanship you cannot see the joins. He fastidiously found accurate paints and carefully test-matched the colours, achieving a great result. But this is a drastic step and you wouldn't do it to 'Greeny' or Carl Perkins's Goldtop – that would clearly be erasing history.

Do-it-yourself versus calling in an expert

We all have varying levels of competence in carpentry, electronics and painting. When I obtained my first electric guitar at the age of 15 it was a complete mess. The teacher I bought it from had bought it on a whim in 1962 at the height of the Shadows' popularity. He learned to play *Apache* then consigned the guitar to a damp attic. When he retrieved it in 1966, 50 per cent of the metal parts were rusted red to the point where none of the saddles would move and the Klusons had huge gaps in their compliance.

What I did next as an innocent 15-year-old is testament to enthusiasm over experience and serves as a good list of 'do nots':

■ I completely disassembled the guitar, paying no attention to what came from where. Take guitars apart carefully and note where everything comes from, especially the screws, which come in many different sizes.

■ I replaced all the rusty screws with the wrong type of replacements. Phillips-type screws were virtually unknown in mid-'60s Britain, but exact replacements are now easily available from many websites.

■ I over-oiled the rusty Klusons thinking they would repair themselves – they didn't, and what's more the excess oil found its way into the neck grain! Again, Kluson replicas are now easily obtained.

When not to respray

Never be tempted to respray a '50s, '60s or '70s Les Paul. However tatty it may have become it's worth more in its original state. Again it's like the 'bruises' on a piece of Chippendale furniture – they are a testimony to the artefact's history. The same, of course, applies to younger Les Pauls, but somehow they don't resonate with quite the same history (yet!).

■ I replaced the bridge with proper American replacements. These cost a fortune and took six months to arrive from California by ship! Now a websearch would replace them in 48 hours.

■ I rewired the electronics to obtain my favourite pickup combinations. Not fatal, but I failed to protect the pickups and capacitors with a heat sink and could have done a lot of damage.

■ I cleaned the volume and tone knobs so well I bleached off the numbers. I replaced a missing knob with a white and gold one – all that Frank Hessy's in Liverpool could offer.

Despite all this the guitar sounded great! I have it on record. However, it was never in tune. The combination of lost neck shims, a poor understanding of the saddle arrangement, rusty Klusons and a poorly set up tremolo/vibrato meant it drove me nuts – so much so that I sold it for £90 (a fortune in 1969 and a 50 per cent profit on the £60 I paid for it). I don't want to know its present value, thank you very much.

This book is driven by the desire to help others avoid my youthful errors.

So bottom line, if you are good with tools and prepared to be diligent and extremely careful, you can probably do most of what this manual expounds and either maintain a lovely instrument in peak performance or radically improve a budget Epiphone.

However if you have any doubt at all about your abilities call an expert. In 1965 there were no guitar techs (not even for Eric Clapton), only luthiers, who all regarded my guitar as a bit of a joke. Today there are at least half a dozen skilled techs in every major city in the world and they all have a sneaking regard for the old warhorses that keep bouncing back.

Never

■ Practise refretting on a vintage instrument. Buy a budget Epiphone and learn the craft first.

■ Attempt a respray unless you have all the required tools and skills and a dust-free environment. Always wear protective mask and clothing.

■ Force the wrong size screw in a body or component.

■ Always protect the guitar surfaces during any maintenance or lubrication.

But whatever else you do, enjoy that special piece of popular music history by playing it every day and trying very hard to wear it out!

I have seen and played a lot of guitars in the last 40 years and I have this thought to pass on:

A well set up budget Epiphone is a better working instrument than a poorly set up Custom Shop '58. In crude terms, a good working Les Paul is about 70 per cent set-up and 20 per cent the synergy of the parts – all pieces of wood are different and even machined metal parts vary in their composition and microscopic detail. The last 10 per cent is alchemy. A good guitar is a good guitar whether old or new.

Does a guitar respond to being played well? Does the prevalent temperature and humidity affect a guitar's sound? *Great* guitars still have a certain mystery about them – long may it remain.

> ### ✎ Tech Tip
>
> There is no such thing as one perfect set-up – what's right for Mark Knopfler is not right for Eric Clapton – so seek your own ideal set-up.
>
> *Glenn Saggers – Mark Knopfler's guitar tech*

Stageside repairs

Given that the electric guitar needs some setting up, it's worth arriving at a gig at least one hour before showtime. This allows for sound-checks and time for the things that go wrong to be put right. Sound-checks give the PA man a chance to serve your needs better – to understand the likely combinations of instruments and any instrument changes during your set. Sound-checks are also great for fault-finding, and time to find solutions.

1 No sound from your guitar?

Step 1

■ Work systematically through the cable chain starting at the guitar, as this is very unlikely to have failed completely.

■ Try changing the pickup selector to another pickup. Is the volume control turned up?

■ Still no sound? Try replacing the cable between the guitar and the amplifier with a new cable (one you are sure is working).

■ The above step bypasses and eliminates any effects chain.

■ If you have sound then try reinserting the effects chain. (Still no sound? Go to Step 2.)

■ If you have sound then you merely had a faulty cable, the most common cause of onstage sound failure.

■ If the sound fails again then it would seem some component of the effects chain is faulty – work through the chain replacing one cable at a time and hopefully isolating the fault.

■ If cable replacement doesn't solve the problem try systematically removing one effect at a time from the chain.

■ If you find a 'dead' component of the chain try replacing the associated battery or power supply.

Step 2

■ Still no sound, even though you are now plugged directly into the amplifier with a 'new' cable?

■ The likely scenario is a 'failed' amplifier. Try checking the obvious causes such as:

– Has the volume been inadvertently turned down to zero?
– Check the master volume and channel gain.
– Is the standby switch in the ON position?
– Does the mains light (if fitted) show 'ON'?
– Is the amplifier plugged in to the mains? Is the mains switched on? Does the stage have a separate fuse?
– Are other amplifiers on the same circuit working?

■ If yours is the only failed amp look to the fuses. There are likely to be fuses on the amplifier (usually a screw-type fuse cartridge near the mains switch). There may also be fuses in the mains plug. Try a replacement.

■ If all of this fails then you must assume the amplifier has a major fault and try a 'work around' – eg sharing an amplifier with the other musicians, etc.

■ The crucial thing here is to be systematic – work through the chain logically, eliminating elements of the chain until the fault is isolated.

2 The guitar won't stay in tune?

Strings!

The most likely cause of tuning difficulties on an otherwise well-maintained guitar is poor or worn strings. The bad news is that changing strings one hour before a gig is also a formula for disaster, as the strings really need time to settle. In an emergency try replacing any individual strings that seem particularly troublesome – rusty first, second and third strings will inevitably cause severe tuning problems.

Loose components?

■ Have the neck securing screws worked loose (Special 2 only)? A quarter-turn can improve the neck stability.

■ Are the machine heads loose?

NB: A machine head that is securely fitted but turns without altering pitch needs replacement. In practice this is unlikely to happen suddenly and should be picked up during routine maintenance.

■ If the guitar has a Bigsby fitted is it poorly set up? This is unlikely to respond to a quick fix. See 'The Paul Bigsby vibrato' maintenance, page 42.

In practice any loose component in the string path will cause instability and hence tuning problems – examine the guitar for loose screws and lost or corroded securing springs. If the strings are OK and there are no obvious loose components then perhaps you have changed string gauges without realigning the guitar?

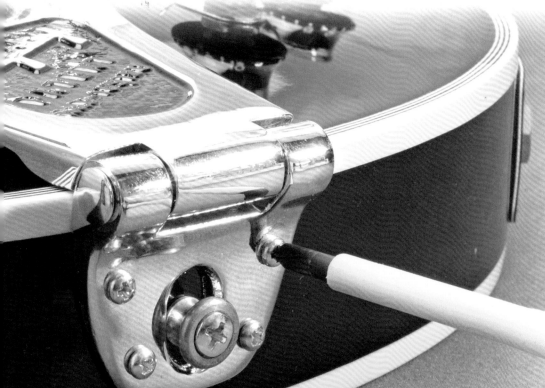

Three-monthly checks

Inspired by an iconic guitarist and realised by a team of craftsman luthiers, the Les Paul is a fascinating hybrid of tradition and innovation. The evolved Les Paul of the late '50s is a great rock survivor. Deceptively rugged in appearance, it is actually easily demolished and when not in use requires a good guitar stand to avoid the danger of taking a disastrous neck-breaking tumble. Otherwise it is mechanically sound, but like all axes repays an occasional sharpening.

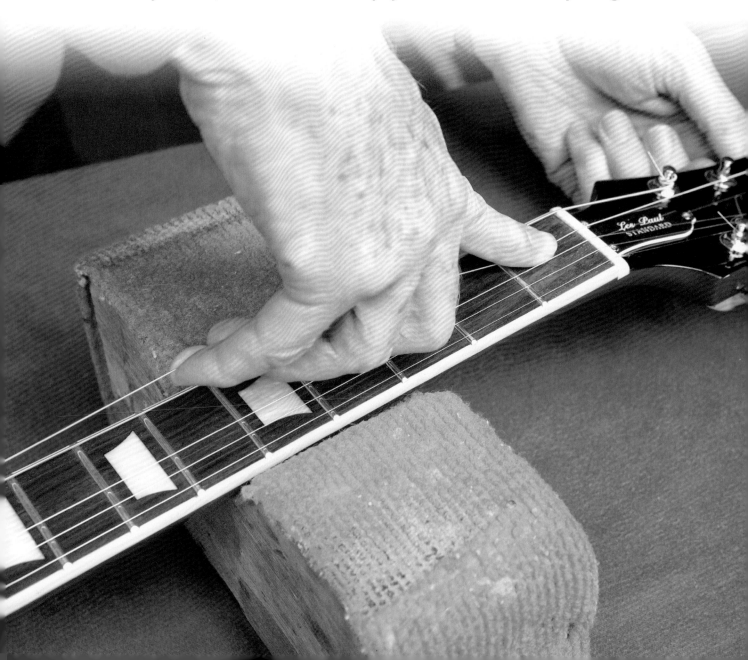

Strings

Change these according to use, at least weekly if you're a gigging professional and at least every three months for students. Use the same brand consistently and use the same gauge and metal type, as this will save time-consuming adjustments to the action and intonation. Different strings have different tensions and gauges can vary from heavy to extra light. Cheap strings are generally a false economy – they are inconsistent and wear out quicker.

A good 'benchmark' in stringing a Les Paul is .010 (1st) to .046 (6th) – light gauge strings for flexibility, but not *too* light. Experiment around this area for your own sound. Les Paul achieved his distinctive early sound with much heavier strings, but that was in an era before much 'string bending' activity.

More recently Joe Walsh has used heavier strings to achieve a distinctive tone. Some heavy metal and 'shred' guitarists use strings lighter than .010s. Experiment, but refer to *'Setting up and tuning', page 35,* to ensure your guitar is adjusted to cope.

New strings are consistent in their profile and hence more 'harmonically correct' along their length – this makes them easier to tune. Old strings are worn by fret contact, are inconsistent and above all sound dull.

Keep new strings sounding good longer by wiping them after every use with a lint-free cloth. This removes corrosive perspiration and prevents premature rusting.

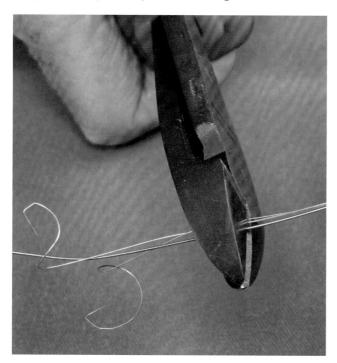

Early Gibsons came fitted with burnished strings and some players even fitted flat-wound strings of a type more usually associated with mainstream jazz styles. Today's fashionable guitar sounds tend to be bright and crisp and this is best achieved with conventional roundwound strings, usually made of nickel wound on steel. Stainless steel is another long-lasting option, though beware of using strings that are made of a material harder than your frets, as inevitably this will result in quicker fret wear.

'Coated strings' are more resistant to corrosion though initially more expensive.

Always use electric guitar strings. This sounds obvious but acoustic guitar strings are not designed for magnetic pickups and are therefore not always magnetically consistent – electric strings are! Stick to one brand as these will be balanced across the gauges both physically and magnetically. If you want to hear the results of acoustic strings on an electric guitar listen to the 1946 Django Reinhardt sessions – even Django struggled to get a consistent response.

To reduce string breakage lubricate any metal string/ saddle contact point. Do this every time you change your strings. The lubricant acts as an insulator against moisture, and reduces friction and metal fatigue. 3-in-1 oil should be applied very, very sparingly to a metal saddle, and graphite to a plastic or bone saddle.

x

Stringing a Les Paul

■ If your tuning keys have a screw on the end of the button as with most Grovers, check the tightness of the screw, as this controls the tension of the gears inside the tuning keys. You should slacken this tension for ease of restringing.

■ As a rule you should change strings one at a time, maintaining an even tension on the neck and thus avoiding any movement in the neck angle.

■ When removing old strings, cutting off the curly ends will assist their passage through the stop tail bridge.

✎ Tech Tip

On vintage-type Les Pauls the stop tail and the ABR-1 Tune-O-Matic bridge are held in place by the string tension – avoid damage to your guitar finish by using a couple of rubber bands to hold these in place whenever you need to remove all the strings.

Frank Marvel

✎ Tech Tip

After stringing it is very important not to over-tighten the machine head locking screws. They should be tightened only to 'finger-tight'.

Frank Marvel

1 Thread the string through the stop tail and insert it into the centre hole in the tuning key.

2 In order to reduce string slippage at the tuning key, I recommend that you use a tie technique. This is accomplished by pulling the string through the keyhole, then pulling the string clockwise underneath itself and bringing it back over the top of itself, creating a knot.

Do this under tension and leave just enough string to achieve a few turnings on the machine head barrel. Wind neatly in a downward pattern – carefully, so as to prevent overlapping the windings. Keep the string under tension with your fingers.

3 Repeat the procedure as above. Note that the bass strings on the left side of the headstock require a clockwise tie and the treble three strings on the right side require an anti-clockwise tie.

4 Crimp any excess string with wire cutters.

Repairing or replacing a jack socket

Heavy use may result in the jack socket spring retainer becoming loose. This can sometimes be easily solved.

1 Remove the four Phillips '1' point screws attaching the jack socket.

2 A gentle squeeze of the 'earth' springed connector may suffice to give a little more tension to the socket.

■ If the jack still seems a little loose then it's worth replacing it with a high-quality guitar-type socket – one that is designed to take regular use. It's worth paying a little extra for a quality component which won't let you down in a pressured stage environment.

3 Removing the old socket first by loosening the retaining nut with a (12mm) socket spanner avoids possible heat damage to the plastic retaining panel.

4 There should be no need to label the two wires – just remember the single core is 'hot' or 'tip' and the screened/braided wire the earth or return, and then carefully unsolder.

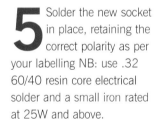

5 Solder the new socket in place, retaining the correct polarity as per your labelling NB: use .32 60/40 resin core electrical solder and a small iron rated at 25W and above.

6 Re-bolt the new jack in place and replace the four Phillips screws on the mounting plate. Take care not to twist the wires.

Tremolo/Vibrato

The trem should be silent in operation, with no 'spring pings'. For adjustment and lubrication, *see 'The Paul Bigsby vibrato' maintenance, page 42*.

Fingerboard wear

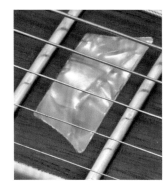

Check for fingerboard wear. Superficial wear is not in itself a problem, but any dips or grooves in the wood will need the attention of a professional luthier, as removing and replacing the neck binding is strictly a craftsman's skill. *See 'Lacquer repairs and fret dressing', page 70*.

Action

Check the action height with the car feeler gauge (.002–.025), applying Gibson recommended specifications:

Neck radius	String height Bass side	String height Treble side
9.5in to 12in	5/64in	3/64in

For details of your specific Les Paul neck radius refer to the case studies section of this book.

If the action is too high or two low, *see 'Setting up and tuning', page 35*.

Volume and tone controls

Check these for electrical crackles and 'dead spots'. If these problems are present then the pots may respond to a treatment with switch cleaner. *See 'Volume controls', page 84*.

Loose strap retainers

A simple problem that can cause havoc if the guitar is eventually dropped! If the retaining screw is loose when fully tightened a cocktail stick or split matchstick will work effectively as a rawlplug.

Pingy strings?

Check for a pinging noise whilst tuning each individual string. This is often caused by the string sticking in the nut grooves at the top of the neck. A light lubrication of graphite dust or silicone projected into the grooves will usually solve this annoying problem and even help tuning stability. A cocktail stick can be used both to mix a little Vaseline and locksmiths' graphite and apply it to the nut grooves. Less serious cases often respond to a simple run with a pencil lead.

Lubrication

One of the most important elements in ensuring tuning stability and reducing string breakage is lubricating all of the contact points of a string's travel. This particularly applies when heavy use is made of any vibrato arm.

A fret polish

Budget Epiphones sometimes arrive with rather unfinished frets. They are workable but feel a little rough, especially when 'bending' strings. The solution is a little simple polishing.

1 After removing the strings mask the fretboard with some masking tape.

2 Wearing protective gloves and eye protection, carefully dress the frets with some OOO grade wire wool. Beware of overdoing this, as you can change the shape of the frets and cause much worse problems. Remove the masking tape.

3 A light application of a little lemon oil will restore the finish on a rosewood fingerboard and also help remove any adhesive deposit left by the tape.

■ An alternative approach

D'Addario, the renowned stringmakers, have recently come up with an alternative solution which saves a little time. They offer a simple card fingerboard mask which literally masks the fingerboard whilst you polish the frets with their supplied light abrasive paper.

String breakage

The foremost contributor to this is moisture collection at the point of contact on the bridge saddle. This can be attributed to the moisture and acidity that transfers from your hands or can be a direct effect of humidity in the air.

■ Metal conflict

Metal-to-metal friction and fatigue is a scientific fact that affects any mechanical device employing a combination of metal materials.

Different metal components, in contact over a period of time, react to each other and break down the integrity of, for instance, guitar strings. A stronger metal will always attack a softer metal (this is why a stainless-steel string may wear a groove into a metal saddle). Finally, you will also find that different string brands will break at different points of tension, due to the metal make-up and string manufacturing techniques.

One of the ways to reduce string breakage is to lubricate the string/saddle contact point with a light machine oil (3-in-1 oil, which also contains anti-rust and anti-corrosive properties, is ideal). The oil acts not only as an insulator against moisture, but also reduces friction and metal fatigue. This lubrication needs to be done sparingly. Use a matchstick or 'Q'-tip end to transfer a minimum of oil to each bridge saddle.

Earthing and RF induction issues

The electric guitar, can be prone to a lot of 'Rattle and Hum'. There are steps that can be taken to improve matters.

The historical perspective

In the 1950s Gibson's customers were playing bars, lounges and small dance halls. Early electric blues players such as Hubert Sumlin were playing in small clubs with no PA system and no stage lighting. In these conditions an unscreened and electrically 'unbalanced' single coil P90 pickup was no real problem. If the player heard a little hum from his amp he could just shift around a little until his pickup was 'off axis' to the hum-generating radio frequencies emanating from his valve amp's huge transformers.

By 1957 this situation was changing, as artists like Carl Perkins might play theatres and even some television shows. The lighting dimmers in such situations often induced a lot of hum into audio circuits, and not just at the low 50–60Hz frequencies that were easily 'lost in the mix'. Soon audiences were hearing nasty 'spikes' in the vocal frequencies where our ears are most sensitive.

The early PA pioneers were drawn towards 'balanced' line audio circuits with their 'hum bucking' properties, but guitarists were left with a growing noise problem.

Today popular music of all kinds has gravitated to stadiums and auditoria bristling with hundreds of computer-programmed lighting dimmers, electric server-driven lighting changes, smoke machines, radio microphones, intercoms and millions of watts of amplification putting every tiny buzz and hum under a microscope.

Humbucking guitar pickups are a part solution but they do sound different. Many guitarists prefer the classic character of electrically 'unbalanced' single coil pickups such as P90s. In search of a solution, as early as 1960 Gibson started experimenting with 'screened' enclosures for some of the guitar cavities.

The screening concept is to build a metallic 'shield' around sensitive 'unbalanced' guitar circuits and connect that screen to an earth potential. The screen effectively intercepts any interference – noise – and drains it away to earth before it can affect the signal passing along the guitar circuits.

Supplementary screening

One part solution to induced hum suggested by guitar craftsman John Diggins is a screening foil applied in the pickup cavities. John uses Stewmac self-adhesive foil (see *Useful contacts* appendix) but also advises that it won't completely solve the problem in today's increasingly electronically 'busy' world.

SAFETY FIRST: Always use eye protection when working with adhesives and solvents.

1 Carefully remove the cover from the cavity you intend to screen. Keep all the screws together in a series of pots and trays – it's worth labelling these NOW, as putting the wrong screws back in the wrong holes will inevitably cause problems.

⬛ Tech Tip

Whenever laying a Les Paul on its front, first remove the three-way switch knob as it often gets strained and broken in this position.

John Diggins – Luthier

2 Turn the guitar over and remove the control knobs – the 'duster solution' is the safest way to avoid damage.

3 Using an 11mm (applies to this Epiphone) socket spanner, remove the nuts retaining the volume and tone pots.

4 Label the pots' positions for ease of reinstallation. It's usually worth drawing a simple diagram to remind yourself of what came from where.

5 You'll need to remove the jack socket if you're screening the control cavity. This Epiphone requires a 12mm socket spanner.

6 Carefully bundle up the labelled cables and still connected pots and tape them together. A small bubble-wrap bag protects the controls and the guitar surface.

7 Carefully prepare the surfaces, removing any grease or rough woodwork that may hamper the adhesion of the foil.

8 First line the sides of the cavity. Trim the foil to size *before* removing the backing tape from the self-adhesive foil.

9 To get an accurate fit for the bottom of the cavity the shape can be impressed on the foil using the top of the cavity as a guide.

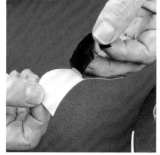

10 The bottom foil is slightly overlapped to ensure good conductivity. On some surfaces the self-adhesive may require a little help and double-sided tape sometimes works. Any surplus copper is trimmed with a safety razor blade.

11 A thin copper strip overlapping the cavity rebate ensures continuity to the back of the cover plate.

67

GIBSON LES PAUL MANUAL

12 Line the back of the control plate cover. A gentle file helps to trim the edges.

WARNING: This foil will be a very effective conductor, so be careful to only apply it where a route to earth or ground is desirable. A bit of foil in the wrong place, which on reassembly touches a 'hot' wire, can short circuit the guitar.

13 A little solder can help ensure continuity at any joins in the foil. When soldering, a dab of 'tinner cleaner' RS561 533 will improve the conductivity of the soldering iron heat and aid a quicker, more effective solder joint.

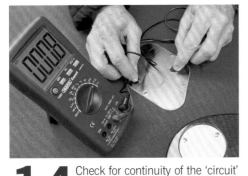

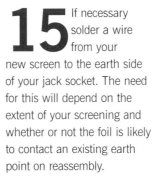

15 If necessary solder a wire from your new screen to the earth side of your jack socket. The need for this will depend on the extent of your screening and whether or not the foil is likely to contact an existing earth point on reassembly.

14 Check for continuity of the 'circuit' created by your new screen. The easiest way to do this is by placing your multimeter prongs at several spaced points on the foil and checking the continuity you've achieved.

16 Holes need to be carefully cut in the foil to allow for reinstallation of the pots.

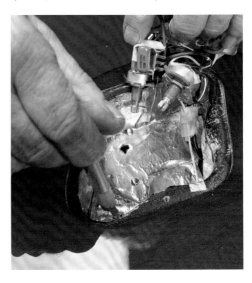

17 Carefully reassemble the control assembly, checking for all points of contact with the new screened surface. All pickups and potentiometers (volume/tone) and switches must be clear of contact with the new surface. A little cloth-backed tape can be an effective insulator.

18 The completed job with all the pots repositioned according to your labelling.

Guitar leads as aerials

As well as noise induced into the pickups guitarists have increasingly long guitar leads to contend with. A long length of 'unbalanced' guitar lead can act as a giant aerial, picking up all sorts of electrical noise and radio frequencies (RF), all of which will be amplified just as effectively as any audio signal running down the line. We have all been to a gig where you suddenly hear taxi radios and ambulance messages blaring through the PA. This is usually the result of RF picked up by unbalanced guitar pickups or leads. Better screening can sometimes help.

Mains hum

In order to reduce induction at 50–60Hz mains hum, it's very important to route *all* your audio cables (guitar FX and microphones) physically away from the mains cables from your gear, as well as elements such as power amplifiers and external power supplies (wall warts). A good rule of thumb is, when an audio cable *has* to cross the path of a mains cable, make sure it crosses at a right angle – this minimises the induction of this type of hum.

Earth loops

An even more common source of hum is the infamous earth loop, also known as a 'ground loop'. These are often difficult to track down and isolate. However, once you've applied most of the common-sense measures to reduce hum, any hum remaining will usually be attributable to a ground loop. It is possible to completely eliminate earth loops if you take the necessary steps, but it involves a systematic process of eliminating problems one component at a time.

■ So what is an earth loop?

Earth loops occur because most modern equipment is fitted with three-pin mains plugs. The third pin on the plug connects the chassis of your gear to AC earth, which ensures that your body cannot become the earth path for AC current. All well and good.

However, when two pieces of equipment both have three-pin plugs and are connected together with cable, the shielding on the cable is also responsible for 'grounding', and an earth loop is possible.

What we now have is two paths to earth (one through its own AC cable; the other through the audio cable connected to the other unit, and consequently through *that* unit's AC cable). Thus a loop of current is formed that can act like an aerial, perfect for inducing hum. You can even pick up radio interference this way as you have effectively created a 'tuned circuit'. If you were doing this on purpose you would call it a radio, but Marconi beat you to it!

■ Troubleshooting

Most earth loop problems can be solved by plugging all of your stage gear into a single earthed AC outlet. However, it's easily possible to overload the AC outlet, so make sure the AC source is rated to handle all the gear you have plugged into it. A guitar amp itself and a couple of FX will certainly be less than the UK-standard 13 amps, but beware of plugging the whole band into one socket! And remember that different countries have different standards or ratings for AC outlets. It's in the interests of your safety to know these.

The only way of being sure you have a potential earth loop problem is to listen carefully for a slightly edgy hum as you're assembling, wiring and cabling your system. Have your gear powered and monitor for hum after each audio connection. This way you can quickly determine and isolate the source of the problem.

Once you identify the unit that is causing the hum then you have to find a 'work around'. This may mean a compromise on the number and position of the units in your audio chain.

It's worth physically moving the unit that seems to be causing the problem and trying again. Sometimes the close proximity of items such as mains transformers can be aggravating the induction problem. You can eliminate battery-operated gear, or gear with two-prong adapters, as they cannot contribute to earth loop problems.

■ Earth lift

Some people solve earth loop problems by using a 'lifting' device (three-prong to two-prong adapter) on one of the units, thus breaking the earth route and severing the loop.

However, NB: This is a very dangerous option that should *not* be used. You are negating the safety factor that the AC earth wire provides. If you choose to use three- to two-prong AC adapters, electrocution may result.

■ Isolating transformers

The best (but more expensive) way to fix a persistent earth loop problem is through the use of a transformer. The job of the transformer is to ensure there is no electrical contact between two pieces of equipment, except for the audio signal. Transformers have no earth connection between the input and output connections, thus effectively breaking an earth loop.

When buying transformers for earth loop problems, it's important to realise that the cheaper variety may colour the sound a little due to frequency response irregularities. Buy the best you can afford – it's worth it.

Intermittents

In my experience these are the worst sort of interference as you're never sure if they're 'cured'.

If you hear a buzz that only appears for a short time and at a constant level, you may have a pulse in your mains lines, which can be caused by the switching action of fluorescent lighting, dimmer switches, window air conditioners, or a refrigerator turning on and off. Again it's a matter of working through the possibilities in a systematic way.

If you must share an AC circuit with any of these elements, and if it's a long-term gig, somebody needs to install a proprietary noise-suppressed AC distribution panel, which will give you a clean power supply for your stage.

Lacquer repair and fret dressing

The Les Paul guitar started out as Les Paul and Gibson's answer to the need for a practical working electric guitar. Fifty years later the guitar is a classic icon and if you have an original you should probably resist any temptation to 'tart it up'. What we demonstrate here are a few repairs that might be appropriately undertaken on a budget 'replica'.

John Diggins could build you a mahogany and maple guitar in the Les Paul mould starting from raw blocks of wood, and he often does. These days John's son Andy takes on a lot of the repair duties in their busy workshop, but John is still very 'hands on' in his approach. This is my documentary record of their approach to some fret and bodywork repairs on an Epiphone 'Standard' that has seen a bit of gig life.

We addressed two main areas:

■ An unwanted 'ding' on the sunburst finish.
■ Some uneven fret wear.

Fret *replacement* on a bound fingerboard is a job best left to experts, as removing the binding often results in the need for a complete neck refinish. What we tackle here is the more feasible task of dressing some uneven frets where replacement is not yet necessary.

Sunburst lacquer repairs

Invisible repairs to the finish on a 'burst is a skilled job. Here's how John approached the challenge.

NB: We would always recommend using a facemask and eye protection when spraying cellulose lacquer.

1 The top bout of this Epiphone has suffered a little altercation with a blunt instrument.

2 For an even spray finish in this area John removed the bridge posts. These are often quite solidly fixed due to wood shrinkage and John employed his own gadget, consisting of a cushioned metal ring and a washer. This acts as a protective conduit, preventing damage to the guitar surface. A proprietary version sold as a 'Knob and bushing puller' is available from stewmac.com (see *Useful contacts* appendix).

3 Having stripped the guitar of fixtures, the surface is prepared with a fine grade freecut paper.

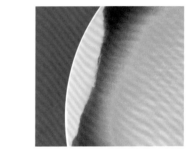

4 The dark outer rim lacquer is then carefully applied with a fine spray in a clean, dust-free environment – note the extractor system.

5 Once the dark coat is dry a clearer diluted colour lacquer is then sprayed, working towards the body of the guitar.

6 Having been allowed to dry once more a clear coat of lacquer is sprayed over the finish.

7 Once thoroughly dry (24 hours) the finish is buffed to a professional sheen. The finish blends in well.

A fret dress and polish

Budget imported Epiphones often arrive with rather unfinished frets. They're workable but feel a little rough, especially when 'bending' strings. Sometimes this is more pronounced, with one or two frets protruding a little over-height, and this involves a little corrective 'dressing'.

1 John Diggins first identifies the offending frets using a straight-edge – the edge will rock on the fulcrum point of any over-height frets. John assesses the frets at left, centre and right.

2 In this particular case John decided to also take a bit of the relief out of the neck by tightening the truss rod.

A little simple polishing

1 After removing the strings John decides not to mask the fretboard, as this also needs a polish. If the board is OK mask the fretboard with some masking tape.

2 Wearing protective gloves and eye protection, carefully smooth the frets with some 320 grade free cut paper. Beware of overdoing this, as you can change the shape of the frets and cause much worse problems. Remove the masking tape.

3 A diamond-edged fret-levelling stone is then used to even out the frets.

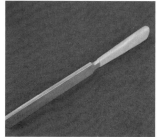

3 John has the facility to buff the frets and fingerboard on an industrial-size buffing wheel. You could do this with a discarded leather guitar strap, impregnated on the soft side with a metal polish and attached to a wooden batton.

■ A light application of a little lemon oil will restore the finish on a rosewood fingerboard and also help remove any adhesive deposit left by the masking tape.

4 A specialised hollow-edged fret file is then used to reshape the crown of the frets.

The above steps apply to worst-case scenarios. Those below apply in most less serious cases:

A Les Paul neck repair

The Achilles heel of this great rock veteran is the headstock/neck area. The great repairer and luthier John Diggins reckons he sees one Les Paul a month sans neck!

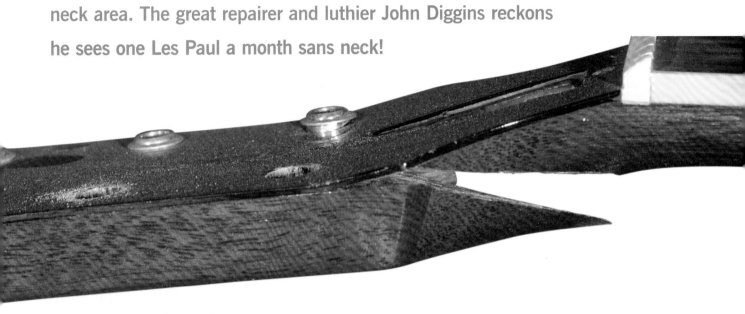

The reason is a combination of factors, including the guitar's weight and the desirability of a slim neck for ease of playing. Gibson experimented during the 1970s with a protruding strengthening volute in this area – which seems to have worked, as John sees few of these guitars. However, nobody liked the extra chunk of wood under their palm so Gibson soon reverted to the slim '60s profile.

The illustration shows the typical 'sprung' nature of the break. The neck itself tends to break cleanly, but the headstock front veneer keeps the guitar together – though a crease often appears in the veneer at the break point.

John's apprentice son Andrew, now a fully-fledged luthier himself, is our guide to a typical and effective repair. He stresses, however, that a very valuable guitar is best left to the experts unless you have a thorough competence in woodwork and a suitable workshop.

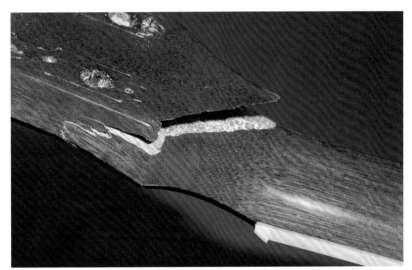

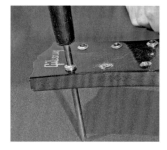 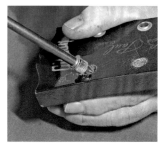  

1 The neck is stripped of all hardware including the machine head ferules – these are often stuck fast due to wood shrinkage, but a clockwise waggle with a snug-fitting screwdriver shank often does the trick.

2 Titebond brand original Aliphatic wood glue is applied well into the break. This glue has a 30-minute setting time but benefits from being left for 24 hours when used at such a critical stress point. The glue is aided into the extremes of the break by a combination of gravity and a lollipop-stick spatula.

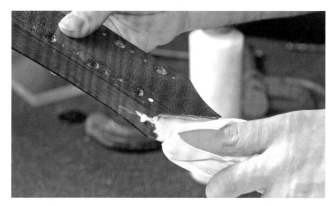 

3 Any excess glue is wiped off to reveal a successful join.

4 Any crease in the fibreboard veneer is minimised by applying a strong half-inch thick perspex splint panel to the front of the headstock – the clear perspex enables inspection of the work during glue setting. It is important not to over-tighten the G clamps here as they could distort the join and leave a mark. Any damage to the back of the headstock is avoided by use of a rubber pad on the clamp jaw.

5 Three clamps are eventually applied, ensuring an even distribution of pressure.

6 Removing the clamps after 24 hours' drying enables a check of the strength of the bond, which is usually stronger than the wood.

7 In order to disguise the break and leave the guitar looking 'as new' it is best to break down the old lacquer with some Nitromors or similar paint stripper, applied with a brush. It is *crucial* that none of the Nitromors seeps through the machine head holes, thus damaging the headstock front!

8 After a few minutes a thin metal woodworkers' cabinet scraper is used to remove the damaged lacquer and also a considerable part of the adjoining surface. Andrew is very careful to avoid raising the lip of the new joint!

9 The neck is sanded smooth (180 freecut) removing any unwanted lacquer in preparation for grain filling.

10 As per the original finish the exposed wood grain is filled with Brummer water-based filler. This is thinned to enable application with a rag, which forces the filler into the grain. Leave for 2 hours. **NB**: A dark filler is used to enhance the grain.

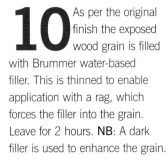

11 When dry, the filler is sanded off the wood in preparation for staining.

12 A carefully matched wood stain is applied to the filled grain.

◢ Tech Tip

Water-based fillers are inert and do not react with nitrocellulose – they are also cheaply available from hardware stores.

John Diggins – Luthier

13 The fingerboard and binding are carefully masked in preparation for spraying – Perfection fineline tape is ideal for the narrow binding.

14 John carefully mixes the dark cellulose lacquer for the heel of the neck. This is colour-tested by eye on a scrap piece of similar timber.

15 Once John is happy with the colour this is carefully spayed onto the guitar heel. Note the guitar body is masked with an old polythene bag (pre CMI).

16 A small amount of clear lacquer plus some yellow colouring is added for the remainder of the neck.

17 After drying the neck is finished off with a final layer of clear lacquer.

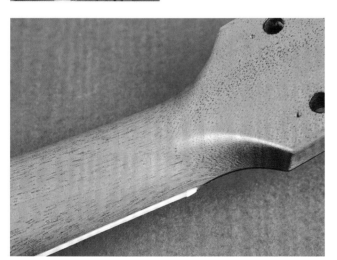

Following all this intense effort the broken Les Paul is returned 'as new', the joint stronger than the original wood. Although John often receives necks that have been rebroken they have invariably broken elsewhere than the previous repair!

Les Paul bridge and stop tail variants

■ In 1952 The Les Paul guitar was originally fitted with a trapeze tailpiece. On the production guitar this featured an impractical 'wrap-under' string arrangement. Curiously the patent for this bridge was filed by Les Paul personally in March '52 and clearly shows he intended a 'wrap-*over*' design. The trapeze was adjustable for height but had no tangible connection to the guitar top, which resulted in lateral movement and intonation problems.

■ In January 1953 Gibson filed a patent for a Ted McCarty stop bar 'wrap-over' design which featured two-point adjustment of height as well as two-point grub screw adjustment of overall string length.

■ In 1952–3 almost 4,000 Les Paul guitars were produced with the above two 'transition' bridges, though the trapeze had been phased out at the end of 1952.

■ Ironically Ted McCarty had filed a patent for the original and then sophisticated Tune-O-Matic ABR1 bridge in July 1952, and this went into production in '53. Initially, however, its use was confined to more expensive 'prestige' models. The upmarket Les Paul 'Custom' of 1954 was deemed worthy of this innovation, which finally arrived on the Goldtop in 1955.

■ Epiphone Les Pauls usually feature a variant Tune-O-Matic bridge with a convenient straight-slot screwdriver height adjustment.

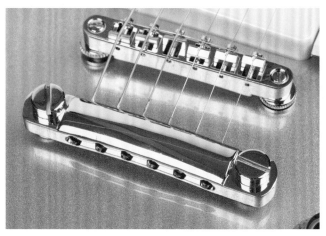

Replacing tuners

Most early Les Pauls were fitted with John Kluson's 1938-patented enclosed tuners. More recently the Grover brand has been adopted for most new Gibson and Epiphone models. Replacement is usually a quite straightforward 'one for one' operation.

I would recommend sticking to Kluson types on any vintage guitar – they're even available with aged 'tulip' tuners to keep the vibe of an old guitar.

Replacing Kluson-type tuners

New look-alikes are manufactured and available from Spertzel and Gotoh. The new tuners have the advantage of a more precise gearing ratio, 15:1 rather than 12:1, and nylon internal washers to take up any slack in the worm gear.

■ First remove the strings (always take the time to reduce the neck tension in a slow and balanced way to reduce the risk of upsetting the balance of the fixed neck).

■ For removal the old Kluson fixing screws require a Phillips '0' or '1' point screwdriver.

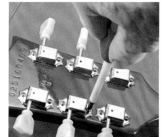

■ When positioning the new machines remember to replace the metal ferrules.

■ Often the new machines will drop straight in.

■ Sometimes the new ferrules are bigger than the originals, and if this is the case you might want to refer any re-drilling to a qualified luthier, especially when working on a rare and valuable guitar.

Replacing Grovers

These are common on many modern Les Pauls, including some Epiphone models. The changing procedure is before, except for the removal of the locking nut, which requires a 10mm socket spanner.

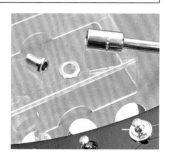

■ The Grover rear screw is another '1' point Phillips.

■ The replacements should drop into place without any need for adjustment to the ferrule holes.

■ Don't forget the washer when replacing the locking ferrule. Tighten the locking nut with a 10mm socket spanner, ensuring a good tight fit – crucial to tuning stability.

Authenticity

Always seek out authentic replacement parts for a vintage guitar. This not only preserves the vintage 'vibe' but also has a huge impact on the resale value of the instrument. Keep the old parts in a labelled bag – they will aid 'provenance' and can be passed on to any subsequent owner.

Pickup replacement

Your Les Paul guitar comes with a 'standard' set of pickups which probably work perfectly well. However, these days guitarists have a lot more sound choices than in 1952.

When the Les Paul guitar was introduced in '52 it came with single coil P90 pickups. In '54 some models came with Seth Lover's Alnico V pickup in the neck position. This had separate magnets for each pole and had a higher output, resulting in an improved signal to noise ratio.

However, with the introduction in 1957 of Seth Lover's wonderful invention the two-wire, patent applied for Humbucker – designed *not* for a different sound but simply to 'buck the hum' – a new era arrived in guitar sound. The noise reduction had been achieved by having two coils in opposite and hum-cancelling phase. But very soon it was realised that the humbucker, by acting *unintentionally* as a 'tuned circuit', considerably altered the sound of the electric guitar. Humbuckers soon became famous for their warmer, more guitar-like sound and it was discovered that their higher output produced interesting overload effects at the input stages of traditional valve amplifiers.

Accidental variance in the wire employed for pickup wiring and the number of windings on the coil resulted in subtle differences, not just in finite output but also in DC resistance and 'resonant peak'. Inductance and capacitance also varied, substantially altering the tuned circuit's effect on frequency response or, in musical terms, tone.

In the 1970s pickup designers seized upon the myriad possibilities for varying this tuned circuit. The factors include the number of windings on a coil, the type of magnet employed, the phase relationship of the coils and that of the two individual pickups.

Pickup guru Seymour Duncan, who owns Seth Lover's original prototype humbucker, started to experiment with the other possibilities presented by two two-coil pickups on one solid-body guitar. 'Four-wire' humbuckers soon appeared with each individual coil having its own output, this presenting another set of possibilities – single-coil sounds from humbuckers and a plethora of parallel and series wiring combinations.

Today's Les Paul owner has enormous choice in the sounds available from a range of 'boutique' and custom wound pickups offered by a plethora of designers. One popular choice is the Seymour Duncan range. These include PAF clones, Alnico 11

magnets, 'jazz' and 'shred' variants as well as one-off custom windings and wirings.

What you choose will depend on the sound you're looking for and I can recommend reading Seymour Duncan's *Pickup Source Book* for inspiration and highly informed insight.

As this manual goes to press Gibson have introduced the 'Push Tone' Les Paul, which has modular 'push-fit' BurstBuckers or P90s. This idea may catch on but until then, whichever pickup you choose for your 'regular' guitar, the practical steps below will apply.

Replacement

For replacement in our Epiphone 'Standard', and following advice from Paul White at Peter Cook's Guitar World, I have chosen Seymour Duncan SH2 'Jazz' Humbuckers in a matched pair, one for the bridge and a slightly different specification for the neck:

Alnico V Bar Magnets

	Neck	Bridge
DC resistance	7.72k	7.90k
Resonant peak	8kHz	7kHz

The relatively high resonant peaks should complement the Epiphone's alder body and maple top. The 'jazz' title refers to the pickup's moderate output and clearer top end response. Seymours recommend this pickup for blues, country and classic rock and describe it as 'the consummate neck humbucker'. The 'four-wire' pickup has been chosen to enable versatility of output wiring – we have included in this book wiring for phase switching and single-coil options from this same guitar, as well as a 'Peter Green' magnet reversal (*see page 96*).

I'm keeping the covers on these pickups because I like the warmer sound that imparts. However, Mike Bloomfield and Jimmy Page preferred them off (just the bridge pickup in Jimmy's case). This alters the 'stray inductance' factor, accentuating the higher frequencies; but we also have EQ available on our amps for that so I decided to protect the fragile coils.

1 De-string the guitar. Release the tension on the neck evenly, *ie* first string, sixth string, fifth string, second string. This is particularly important on a set-neck guitar as neck re-setting is a major and expensive job. If you have Grover machines don't forget to loosen the tension screws before unwinding. An electric string winder attachment is a useful RSI buster. Plug in your soldering iron to warm it up.

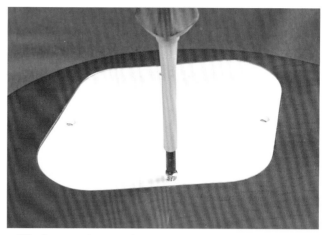

2 Remove the cover from the rear access panel using a '1' point Phillips screwdriver. Use a screw-keep of some kind to avoid lost or mixed up screws – I currently use recycled dental floss containers.

3 Remove the old pickups using the same screwdriver on the four mounting screws located at each corner. Place the mounting blocks to one side as these will fit the replacements perfectly. Note the slimmer mount for the neck pickup and the tapered angle – you will need to retain this orientation on reassembly.

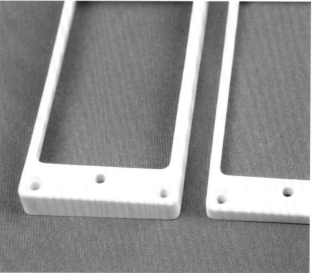

4 Draw yourself a diagram of the pickup wires' position in the existing arrangement. Then carefully snip off or unsolder the old pickup wiring from the existing volume pots. These connections can be identified from the wiring diagram (see right) or simply by gently tugging the pickup wires from the pickup cavity end.

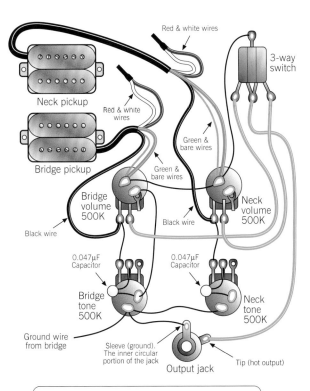

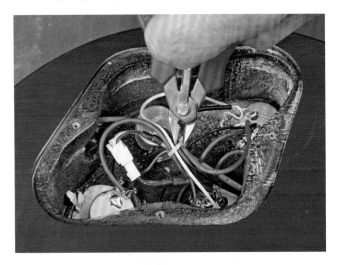

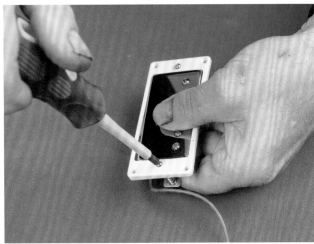

5 Place the new pickups in the mounting blocks, taking care to observe the manufacturers' marked designation of 'neck' and 'bridge' pickup – they are electrically different. Also take care to use the slimmer block for the neck pickup. John Diggins has a useful gizmo for holding the fiddly springs in place, but you can improvise.

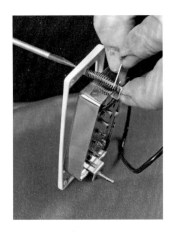

6 Label the new pickup wires clearly, as once they're both in the control cavity they may appear to be the same. Put the neck pickup in place first as this makes wiring simpler. Carefully thread the cables through to the control cavity. Note the orientation of the pole pieces *closest* to the fingerboard when positioning the pickup.

7 Tin the new wires with a little solder and then re-solder these as per your diagram, or see diagram above right as a guide. Replace the rear cavity cover.

Pickup height settings

It seems reasonable to assume that having your pickups set high and therefore closer to the strings will produce more output from your Les Paul and possibly more tone. However, be aware that the magnetic field from either a P90 or a humbucker is strong enough to interfere with the natural excursion of the strings, which can result in very odd harmonic effects. Most notably the sixth string sounded at the 12th fret can produce odd 'beats' and very uneven intonation.

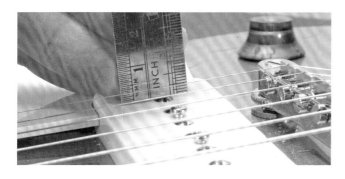

Gibson have an interesting recommendation which is not height specific but based on listening. They suggest that having your pickups set too high will cause a muddy, overly distorted sound; and having them set too low will produce a weak, unfocused sound. So they suggest either leaving the pickups at their 'optimally set' factory height or experimenting by ear until you find the sound that works for you!

1 To establish your current setting, depress all of the strings at the last fret. Using a 6in (150mm) ruler, measure the distance from the bottom of the first and sixth strings to the top of the pole piece. As a rule of thumb, the distance should be greatest at the sixth string, for the neck pickup position, and closest at the first string position.

A guide figure based on factory-set Gibsons would be bridge pickup 3/32in at the sixth string and 1/16in at the first.

In the last analysis you will have to decide for yourself on the most effective compromise between output level, tone and magnetic interference.

Humbucker height recommendations

	Bass side	Treble side
Neck pickup	3/32in	1/16in
Bridge pickup	3/32in	1/16in

2 Using a 4mm straight-slot screwdriver and an accurate metal ruler, adjust the height to the above starting points and then follow Gibson's own idea of adjusting for your sound.

Note how on this factory set 'Standard' the neck humbucker is set considerably lower than you might expect, but this works well, especially when working on the higher frets.

Volume controls

Testing, cleaning and/or replacement of standard 500K pots.

■ So why would you want to do this?

The Les Paul volume and tone controls are carbon-based potentiometers, an invention of the late 19th and early 20th centuries. They're crude and mechanical but they work. They do, however, generate 'dirt' by the nature of the mechanical friction of metal on carbon. This loose carbon inside the pot impedes the electrical contact and often causes it to be intermittent and prone to audible crackling. Corrosion of the metal parts adds 'snap' to the 'crackle'. We shall concentrate here on the volume pots, as due to their more frequent use these are the ones most likely to fail.

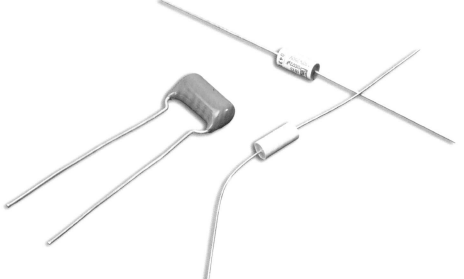

UNDERSTANDING THE RESISTIVE CAPACITOR CIRCUIT
If you alter the resistance of a circuit (in this case by turning your guitar's tone control) and that circuit also has a capacitor in circuit, which it does, the frequency response of that circuit will alter. We perceive this as a change in subjective musical tone.

Testing a pot to see if it is still functional

1 Remove the knob from the suspect pot. Remove the retaining nut with a socket spanner.

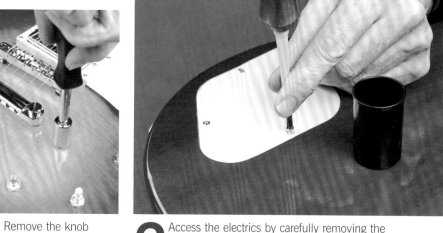

2 Access the electrics by carefully removing the rear control panel cover with a Phillips '1' point screwdriver. Keep the screws together in a small container.

3 Isolate the pot by first labelling then unsoldering the internal wiring. If you're slow with your soldering iron, then use a pair of crocodile clips or something similar as effective 'heat sinks' to draw heat away from other damageable components. John Diggins actually uses a set of surgical forceps that not only draw away heat, but have enough mass to hold things in position if required.

4 Set the multimeter to 'ohms' measurement in the 2M range. Zero the meter. Bring the multimeter probes into contact with the two outer connection prongs. A Les Paul volume or tone control should present a reading of 500K, give or take 20 per cent. In this case on an auto ranging meter we get .489M ohms. A figure higher than this suggests the pot should be replaced.

NB: It's worth checking that the guitar has the correct pots fitted, as with an old guitar they may have been changed at some point. Sometimes the resistance value is marked on the pot casing.

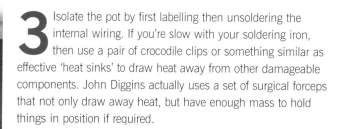

5 If the pot is giving the correct resistance value you can also test the smooth working of the carbon track. Apply one of the multimeter probes to one of the pot's outer prongs and the other to the middle prong. Use crocodile clips to hold the probes in position. The resistance value indicated on the multimeter should smoothly alter as you rotate the pot control. If the needle shows an intermittent response the pot may need cleaning.

6 Repeat the process, this time testing the other outer prong in relation to the middle prong.

Cleaning

Sometimes a well-used pot can be restored to useful service by simple cleaning/lubrication. However, the replacement pots are so cheap and readily available nowadays it's worth considering replacement. Also, 'switch cleaner' works well on switches but less well on carbon pots.

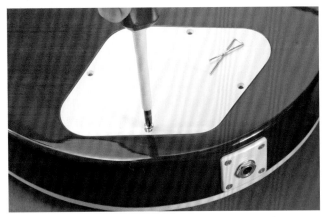

1 Using a Phillips '1' point screwdriver, unscrew the rear panel and keep the screws together in a small container. (The paperclip is handy for getting the panel off, as it's often a tight fit – poke through the screw holes rather than damage the edges.)

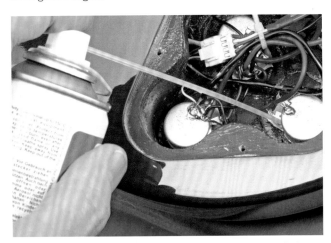

2 Using the supplied hose, squirt a good quality switch or contact cleaner (eg Blue Shower or DeOxit) into the pot through the opening on the side of the case. If the pot is sealed, try cleaning via the microscopic gap around the shaft. You should try if possible to flush out any dirt. Also turn the pot shaft to allow the cleaning fluid to reach all of the contact points. Avoid getting switch cleaner on the guitar surface, and wear safety glasses to protect your eyes. Carefully replace the rear panel and test the cleaned pot.

If you still have noise problems or 'dead spots'

Everything mechanical eventually wears out, so consider a replacement pot. It makes a huge amount of sense to replace with an exact Gibson-specification pot, readily available via the Internet. The type 500K pots are available slightly cheaper from radio supply shops, but all pots are not created equal and you may find slight variances in shaft sizes etc which can cause problems.

Replacing a volume or tone control

NB: This will involve electrical soldering, so protect your eyes with safety glasses and cover any guitar parts that may be spattered by stray solder.

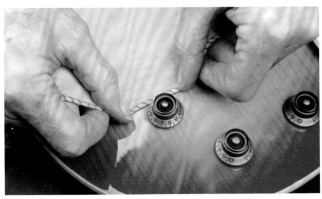

1 Remove the plastic knob from the offending control. These can become quite solidly fixed, so avoid damage to the guitar by using a soft rag wrapped around and under the knob for extra torque.

2 Using a Phillips '1' point screwdriver, unscrew the rear panel and keep the screws together in a small container.

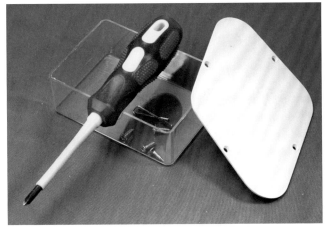

3 Label the cables connected to the old pot with some cloth-backed tape ('cloth-backed' is easy to write on, though a sticky label wrapped back on itself works just as well), assign each cable a number, and draw yourself a little sketch of what goes where, noting the orientation of the tags on the old pot in relationship to the back of the pickguard. This sounds elementary but some old cables are not colour coded and there are alternative wiring options. Taking this approach restores your wiring intact and gets you back to the sound you've come to expect.

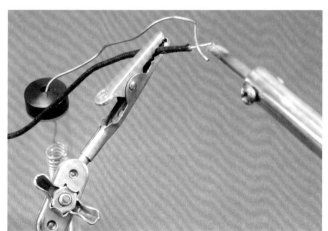

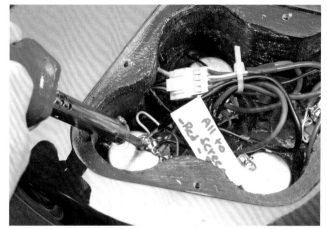

4 Carefully unsolder the old pot with the lowest rating soldering iron you have – 15W may work but a higher rated iron used quickly will be fine.

5 Use a socket-type spanner – the size will vary from model to model (see 'Specific case studies', pages 101–149) – and unbolt the nut retaining the pot to the guitar body. (A socket-type spanner/wrench is less likely to mark the lacquer than a conventional spanner and any abrasion is below the switch skirt.)

6 Place the new pot in position, retaining the old orientation (refer to your diagram), and fix with the new retaining nut, not forgetting the washer.

7 Tin the new connecting wires for the replacement pot with a little solder, and solder them in place as per your labelling. A crocodile-clip stand makes a great 'third hand' for these jobs. A lollipop stick also works as a non-conductive aid and doesn't waste any heat. Reassemble as before.

Nut adjustment

A well set up nut made of a suitable material can radically transform a guitar's performance.

A word of warning

The nut is one of the most difficult and skilled adjustment/replacements for an amateur. Correct nut shaping – which is essential to ensure stable tuning, good tone and correct string spacing – is not a job to be taken lightly. Even if you're buying a pre-formed Les Paul nut you'll need specialist tools to make minor adjustments. If you're at all unsure of your skills or tooling then I recommend you take your Gibson or Epiphone to a qualified guitar tech or luthier.

■ So why would you want to do this adjustment?

Wear in the nut slots perhaps caused by the sawing action of extensive Bigsby use or just tuning and wear and tear, can make the action at the nut/first fret too low, resulting in buzzing and snagging.

Another reason is to perhaps replace a cheap plastic nut with a bone substitute, which has better acoustic properties and is self-lubricating.

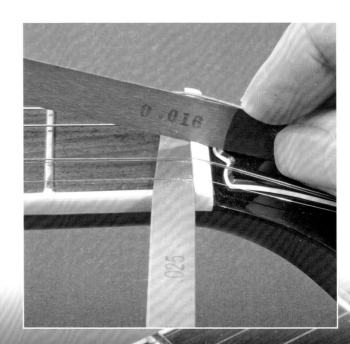

Replacing the nut

1 Remove the strings. Be aware of the loose bridge and tailpiece, which can easily be secured with a couple of rubber bands. There is usually no overlapping polyurethane on a Gibson so just remove the truss rod cover with a Phillips '1' point screwdriver. If you're not a skilled luthier I would recommend protecting the fingerboard and head-stock with several layers of masking tape.

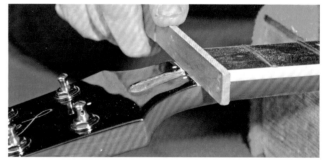

2 Remove the old nut. Tap the nut gently using a small hammer. With luck the nut should eventually become loose and can be removed as one piece reasonably easily. As a last resort prise the nut out with a pair of smooth-ended pliers. The smooth ends will avoid damaging the old nut, which – assuming you were happy with your original string spacing – provides a perfect template for the new spacing.

3 If it is necessary clean the nut slot of any surplus adhesive, lacquer etc. A narrow and sharp file can be used as an effective tool on both the end of the fingerboard and the bottom of the nut slot. A custom file slightly narrower than 3/16in is required.

4 Smooth the nut slot with a specialist 'nut seating file' specific to the Epiphone or Gibson size. It's important to avoid chipping the neck finish, so gently file the sharp edge of any lacquer and also file the nut bottom with inward strokes from both ends of the nut slot, thus avoiding accidentally pulling any lacquer from the neck.

5 Approximate the new nut blank. Begin with an oversize blank, which can then be shaped down to a custom fit. John does this on a grinding wheel but it's OK and safer to work by hand with a file fixed in a regular vice.

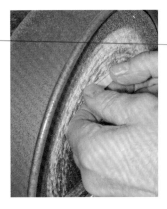

NB: PLEASE use bone or synthetic Micarta, not endangered ivory!

7 Draw the fingerboard outline radius onto the new nut with a sharp pencil.

8 Add a pencil radius above the fingerboard outline. This new radius needs to be enough to account for the fret height, the string height and the thickness of the string (a guitar tech might add a little more for good measure!). You will certainly need to allow a little more height towards the bass strings, as they need more room to vibrate without 'choking' on the first fret.

6 Measure your nut slot width and mark the required nut slots on your new blank based on the precise measurements of your nut slot and your old nut. Ideally you should carefully copy the string spacing from the old nut. Pay particular attention to the spacing of the sixth and first strings from the outside edge. Having strings too close to the edge will make finger vibrato difficult.

■ Check constantly for a snug and even fit in the nut slot. At this juncture the nut should still be left slightly overlong for flexibility at the later stages of shaping. A 1/8in edge overlap will be enough to allow for some fine tuning.

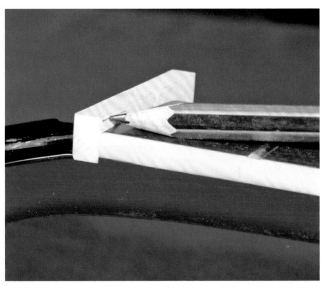

9 You can position the first two outer strings on the new nut by making pilot notches with a very fine craft saw (X-acto or similar, with a blade of .010 gauge or less). If for some reason you don't have the old nut then a specialist tool, a compensated nut spacing template, is the easiest way to get even spacing between the outside of adjoining strings – a more important factor than equal spacing at their centres. Use this or the old nut to determine the position of the remaining string slots.

■ Surprising as it might seem, expert luthiers often determine the individual string spacing by eye. Though this sounds a little unscientific, the precise calculations in thousandths of an inch are made very complex by the fact that each string is a different gauge. (This is where the template can be used for reference.)

■ You can adopt the pro method to a degree by positioning the strings in very shallow 'pilot' slots then making any minor adjustments by eye before completing your filing of the final slots.

10 Carefully file the new slots to the depth marked on the new nut. In practice this can be 'fine tuned' on the guitar.

Specialist precision nut files will allow smoothing of the nut slot bottom without damaging the sides of the slot (see *Useful contacts* appendix). These files have smooth edges and a round bottom and are available in the precise size for your chosen string gauges. In practice a luthier would use a slightly smaller file than the requisite slot and use a rolling technique on the forward motion to widen the slot with more control and less chance of the file snagging. A carefully chosen feeler gauge can be a useful guide whilst filing, preventing any chance of filing too deep. The correct depth for the string slots – which as a rule is slightly more than the fret height – is calculated using a feeler gauge and a straight-edge.

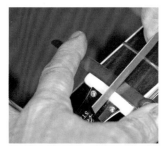

Emergency measures

An alternative to a complete nut replacement, and useful in an emergency – especially if only one or two nut slots are too deep – is to recycle some material from the top of the nut (assuming excess is available) and use this as infilling material.

To do this, tape both sides of the nut with masking tape then take a coarse file and file the top of the nut approximately half the depth you expect to raise the slots. Catch the loose filings on a piece of paper. Fill the offending slots with the loose filings. Then carefully soak the filings with thin superglue. Press the solution into place with a toothpick. When dry, re-file the slots, referring to the methods described above. As before, the slots should be made so the string sits in about half to three-quarters of their diameter, though a Les Paul will cope quite well with deeper nut slots, especially if you're a 'heavy picker'. Slots should taper downwards on the tuner side, and again the strings' first point of contact must be at the fret side of the nut.

File at a back angle, to shape the floor, or bottom, of the slot correctly. This enables the string to slide through freely. If the slot isn't correctly shaped, it will prevent smooth tuning and will hamper the instrument's ability to return to tune, particularly after using a Bigsby vibrato.

When a string binds in the nut slot, it makes a pinging sound as it breaks free. This ping is often attributed to the tremolo/vibrato, as it's the use of this device that triggers the release of the snagging. The nut will eventually need lubricating with graphite (*see 'Tech Tip' above*). The back angle of the slot will give good contact for the string, important for tone, whilst a first contact point at the front (fret end) of the nut will ensure correct intonation. Ideally the bottom of the nut slot should be rounded as per the relevant string radius.

11 Secure the new nut in place with a couple of dabs of glue. Don't overdo the glue, as the nut may need removing again for correction.

12 Check the action at the 1st fret. A feeler gauge at the nut should register approximately .038in but this will naturally depend on the specific fret heights. This figure is arrived at by taking a measurement between the 1st and 2nd frets as shown and adding approx .005in for clearance and also subsequent nut wear.

Rewiring options

Les Paul's wonderful guitar was born out of a restless search for 'the sound I hear in my head'. As part of that quest, most guitarists know about 'The Log', the semi-solid guitar Lester made in the Epiphone factory and eventually took to Gibson as a prototype. However, perhaps more important were his three circa 1941 'Klunkers'.

Congratulations, Les Paul, on winning the Down Beat Guitar Poll. We're proud of the interest in guitars fostered by your artistry, and we're proud, too, of the wonderful Gibsons now under construction for you and Mary. We are confident these fine instruments will inspire you to new feats of wizardry in your musical accomplishments.

GIBSON, INC., Kalamazoo, Michigan

Gibson announced the Les Paul guitar in 1952 by showing Lester playing an 'Epiphone' Klunker!

These 'Klunkers' (Lester loves made-up names) were also Epiphones, but a semi-acoustic model with a trapdoor in the back. Lester loved this trapdoor because he was constantly experimenting with new pickups and pots searching for that elusive sound, and with this facility on the guitar he could make changes *without* removing the strings. That trapdoor lives on in the back of *your* Les Paul.

You may have noticed Les Paul himself plays an odd-looking Les Paul, and one that seems to be in a constant state of evolution – he was still tinkering at 92, still searching, like so many musicians, for that mysterious 'sound in his head'.

Many of us think of the Les Paul as a distinctive but 'one-sound' guitar. However, if we think of Peter Green's 'burst, we think of a different sound, accidentally out of phase – and also Jimmy Page's guitar, with a 'push-pull' pot, very versatile and sometimes surprisingly clean.

In the writing of this book, and with expert help from John Diggins, I opened that little trapdoor and tried a little tinkering myself. What we arrived at is a very surprising and very versatile guitar. I recommend tinkering to any Les Paul owner, except perhaps those with a '59 'burst in mint condition!

Coil tapping

In the section on pickup replacement I recommended a four-wire pickup as a replacement for the normal two-wire found on most stock Les Pauls. This offers great flexibility. One option is to wire the four-wire pickup to be both a humbucker and a single coil, giving you four sounds instead of two from the two pickups on your regular Les Paul. These sounds are the normal 'warm' humbucker plus the brighter sound associated with single coils. This I find a very useful arrangement and when done using 'push-pull' pots need not outwardly affect the look of your guitar.

'Push-pull' pots function exactly like the normal 500K volume or tone pots on your guitar, with the added facility of a switch function achieved by pushing or pulling the pot up or down from the guitar body. Because the tone pots tend to be used less and are further from the normal right-hand playing position I recommend you install the push-pull facility on these pots.

The 'push-pulls' can be obtained from most guitar spares outlets. They're designed to fit directly in place of the original pots with little fuss.

1 Remove the rear control pane using a '1' point Phillips and label the wires attached to your existing tone pots – perhaps even do a drawing of what goes where.

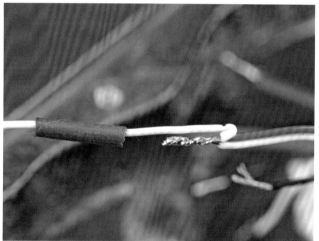

2 Remove the old pots, using a duster to first safely extricate the knob. The pots themselves require a 7/16in socket spanner.

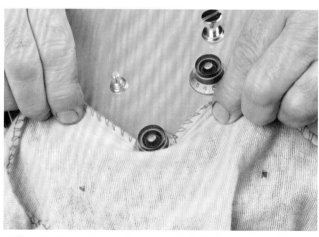

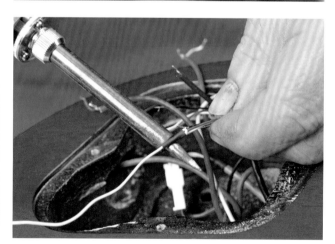

3 You'll need to cut the original labelled wires from the rear of the old pots.

4 In this installation John Diggins extended the four pickup wires to the 'push-pull' pots as the extended wires are far easier to manipulate. He also uses heat-shrink sleeving to insulate the joint. This pulls back over the join and is easily made to fit snugly with the application of a little heat. Use the side of your soldering iron, *not* the tip, when heating the sleeving.

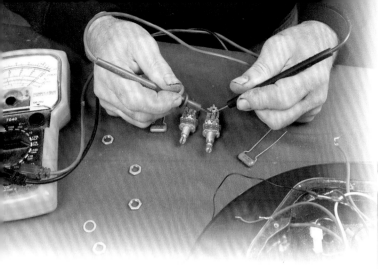

5 John confirmed the direction of switching of the new 'push-pull' pot (which came without any documentation) using a multimeter set to check continuity. This in fact tallies precisely with the very useful diagrams supplied by Seymour Duncan Pickups (see diagram below). This wiring needs to be carefully adhered to.

7 The pickup 'hot' wires are soldered to the existing volume control.

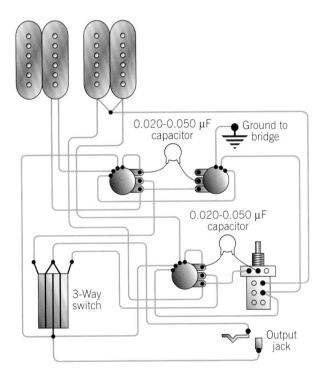

0.020-0.050 µF capacitor

Ground to bridge

0.020-0.050 µF capacitor

3-Way switch

Output jack

8 Then the extended coil 'tap' wires are soldered to the new switch.

9 A 'common' wire is necessary from the new switch to the volume pot case. This wiring when switched 'up' on the pot effectively routes one of the coils to earth and therefore produces a 'single coil' arrangement. Ideally this pot should have the casing routed to earth.

The advantage of this wiring is that when the two pickups are 'on' they are out of phase as per 'Jimmy Page'.

6 For neatness John prefers to replace the existing capacitors and hard-wire them to the case of the new 'push-pull' pot. John also prefers to do the tone control wiring externally to the guitar and then fit the pots.

Tech Tip

The snag with 'push-pull' pots is that the knobs can come off mid-performance! Sometimes 'split' pots can be expanded slightly for a tighter fit. Another solution is a little PTFE tape around the pot shank.

Frank Marvel

Phase reversing the pickup polarities

This gives 'out of phase' tone effects when *both* pickups are selected together. This out-of-phase effect has been used to great effect by both Peter Green and Jimmy Page, though this particular modification is more akin to a Jimmy Page arrangement. See further on for a magnetic phase reversal.

Phase reversal could involve another additional switch – not an aesthetically desirable option, particularly on a vintage guitar, so we have here opted again for a 'push-pull' pot, this time replacing the bridge volume control.

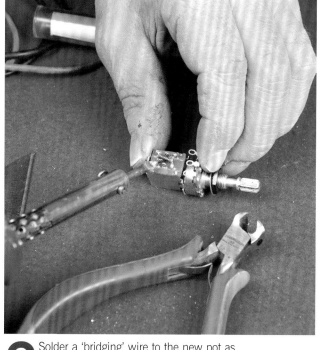

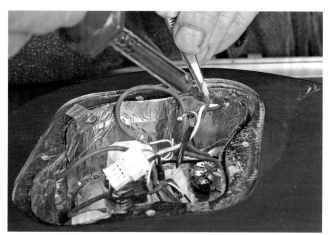

1 Assuming the rear access panel is removed, carefully label the existing wiring to the bridge volume control and unsolder it. Remove the old pot as shown.

2 Solder a 'bridging' wire to the new pot as indicated in the diagram below left.

3 Solder the second bridging wire to the new 'push-pull' pot, as per the diagram.

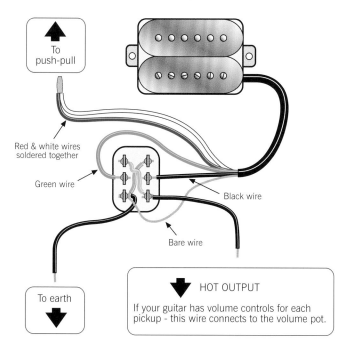

To push-pull

Red & white wires soldered together

Green wire

Black wire

Bare wire

To earth

HOT OUTPUT
If your guitar has volume controls for each pickup - this wire connects to the volume pot.

4 Solder the red 'hot', ground, green and black wires to the new pot as shown in Figure. NB: The 'blue' wire is in fact a screened pair connected to the 'tone' pot, and the red and white are connected together and also route to the tone pot. Reassemble.

A Peter Green effect: magnetic/electronic phase reversal

Many guitarists are intrigued by the distinctive sound of the Les Paul Peter Green played on his late '60's recordings. In the Greeny case study (*see page 148*) I record Jol Dantzig's observation that Peter's Les Paul has a *magnetically* out of phase pickup.

We've already covered putting the bridge pickup *electronically* out of phase with the neck pickup via a 'push-pull' pot. The question remains, however, as to whether magnetic and electronic out of phase relationships *sound* different from each other. I have tried to put this to a scientific test, though in the end the judgement remains largely subjective – sound quality or timbre is very hard to definitively measure.

For our test I used the case study Epiphone 'Standard', now fitted with Seymour Duncan 'Jazz' humbuckers and a push-pull 'phase reverse' switch. To emulate our experiment proceed as shown below.

1 De-string as usual. Take care to 'elastic band' the Tune-O-Matic and stop tail in place – they can easily fall off and do damage to the 'burst.

2 Make a careful note of the pickup height (as this is a significant factor in the sound) and remove the neck pickup using a '1' point Phillips.

3 Remove the pickup surround using a 4mm straight-slot screwdriver. Use a 'keep box' for all the screws and the two pickup height springs.

4 Carefully saw through the solder that attaches the pickup cover to the backplate. This machine solder is too 'high temperature' for the average electrical solder iron and we wish to avoid melting the pickup wax. A small craft saw will do the job. Take care to remove the saw filings – these can cause havoc if allowed inside a pickup.

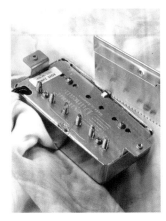

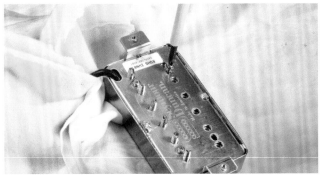

5 Unscrew the pickup backplate using a '0' point Phillips.

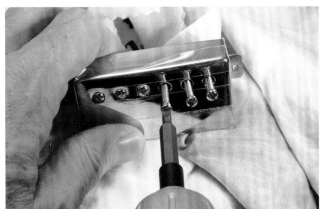

6 On some pickups the adjustable pole pieces may need to be removed, but *only* if their heads are larger than the pickup 'can' holes. This requires a 4mm straight-slot screwdriver.

7 Now carefully tease the pickup from its 'can' – the pickup may be wax dipped and therefore quite a snug fit. Be very gentle, as it is easy to break the internal wiring.

8 The magnet in this instance is loose fitted to the rear of the two pickup bobbins, but sometimes they are secured by a screw.

9 Mark the polarity of the magnet with a felt-tip pen.

10 Reverse North and South by turning the magnet 180°.

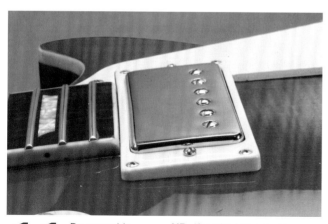

11 Re-assemble the pickup, not forgetting to resolder the 'can' – this is very important, as the 'can' needs to be solidly grounded to earth.

NB: If you're interested in reinserting the pickup backwards as on the original 'Greeny' then you'll need to replace the pickup surround reversed, 'skinny end' to the neck.

Subjective judgements

I recorded the pickup before and after the magnetic phase reversal and on reviewing the recordings came to the following conclusions:

■ The neck pickup alone prior to magnetic reversal sounds terrific – full-blooded, gutsy and with the classic humbucking sound, clean and mean and also capable of a tasteful valve overdrive crunch.
■ When switched *electronically* out of phase with the bridge pickup it sounded a bit 'synthetic' – definitely 'out of phase' but somehow a little clinically so.

After magnet reversal

■ The neck pickup on its own sounds different, as if some EQ has been applied – less LF more high mid-frequencies.
■ Combined electronically 'out of phase' with the bridge pickup the sound is now more 'scooped' and hollow sounding in the mid-frequencies – less synthetic than the purely electronic phase reversal.
■ Combined electronically 'in phase' the sound is still different, fuller and more rounded than previously.

After magnet reversal and with the pickup mounted reversed (adjustable poles nearest the bridge)

I tried this as it's the 'Greeny' set-up.
■ Resulted in a very 'gritty' sound with more high mids.
■ When switched electronically out of phase with the tone pots flat out it sounded very gritty.

Pickup reversed but electronically in phase

■ This sounds like the more conventional 'two pickups on together', some comb filter effects occurring.

Conclusion

In a perfect world this experiment needs to be repeated with PAFs fitted to a '58 'burst – our finances, however, preclude that.

In the circumstances the nearest I could get to Peter's distinctive sound was with both pickups 'on', the neck pickup magnetically 'out of phase', and with the pickup in the 'incorrect' orientation *and* electronically out of phase. So that's magnetically 'out of phase' but 'semi-phase corrected' by pickup re-orientation then 'out of phase' again electronically via a switch! The sound was much enhanced by backing off the guitar volume (on both pickups) and cutting much of the high frequencies with the guitar tone pots.

Needless to say I could not achieve Peter's signature vibrato, timing or phrasing. As so often, I think this is not so much a 'hardware' issue as 'personal software'. As Peter Green famously said of his Les Paul 'It's no magic stick.'

Truss rod adjustment

In 1919 Gibson were the first major instrument manufacturer to install a truss rod. By the mid-1920s they were installing a spoke wire rod in every 'non-Classical' instrument made at their Kalamazoo factory.

A truss rod is made necessary on a steel-strung guitar due to the string-induced force on the neck, which when at pitch is approximately 200lb. The truss rod torque on a typical mahogany neck is 18–22in/lb.

The Vintage Les Paul truss rod adjusts at the headstock and usually requires an 8mm/5/16in socket spanner. Gibson in fact supply a combination Phillips/socket tool with many of their new guitars. A socket spanner with a flexi extension works just as well. The Epiphone Les Pauls require a 4mm Allen key.

The standard truss rod can counteract concave curvature, for example in a neck that has too much relief, by generating a force in the neck opposite to that caused by excessive string tension.

The recommended neck relief for a 12in neck radius is approximately .010in (0.25mm), though this is a very subjective judgement.

NB: For obvious reasons the truss rod was originally conceived to adjust situations with too much relief – it is much more likely to be successful in this application.

■ If you feel unqualified Do NOT attempt any truss rod adjustment on a rare and precious guitar. Talk instead to an experienced guitar tech via your local music shop.

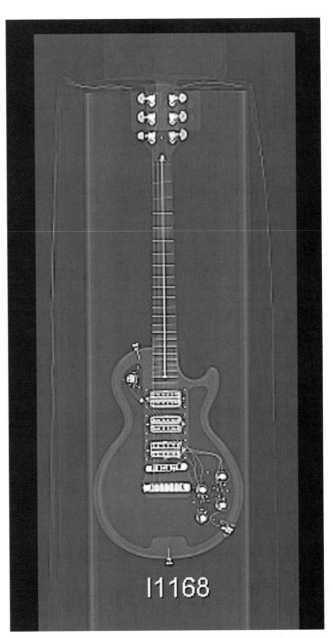

The truss rod on a Peter Frampton Les Paul seen in X-ray – the shot also reveals the semi-acoustic body of this unusual Les Paul..

1 Check your tuning (which should be at standard A440 pitch or your preferred and consistent 'custom pitch'). Install a capo at the 1st fret, depress the sixth string at the last fret.

2 With a feeler gauge, check the gap between the bottom of the sixth string and the top of the 8th fret. If the neck is too concave (indicated by too big a gap measured with the feeler gauge) then you may consider adjusting the truss rod.

3 Access the truss rod adjustment by removing the two Phillips '1' point screws on the 'shield' truss rod access cover.

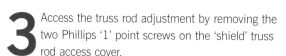

4 Turn the truss rod nut clockwise to remove excess relief. If the neck is too convex (strings too close to the fingerboard), turn the truss rod nut counter-clockwise to allow the string tension to pull more relief into the neck.

Tech Tip

A flat neck without string tension is a good start, so many techs make this adjustment without strings. A 'straight-edge' tool applied to the neck as a reference makes the job simpler.

John Diggins – Luthier

5 Check your tuning, then recheck the gap with the feeler gauge and readjust as necessary.

NB: If you meet excessive resistance when adjusting the truss rod, or your instrument seems to need constant adjustment, or adjusting the truss rod has no effect on the neck, then take the instrument to a qualified guitar tech.

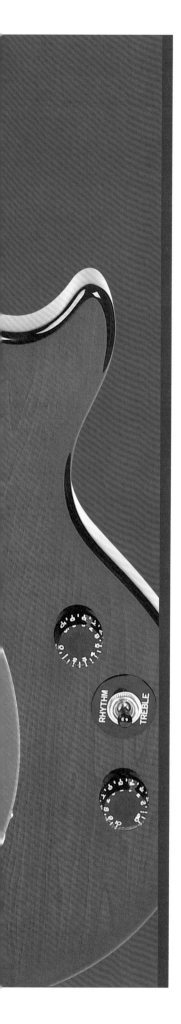

Specific case studies

Over 50-plus years the Les Paul guitar has continued to evolve. Ironically the iconic guitars of 1958–60 are still the high watermark and these are constantly emulated. I cannot hope to cover all the myriad variants that have arisen based on these and the previous Goldtops. However, these generic studies should cover enough details for most routine maintenance and appraisal.

LEFT 55 years of Les Paul innovation.

RIGHT Honeyburst reissue.

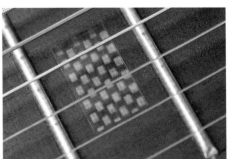

 Case study variants

With notable exceptions, Gibson have preserved their distinctive marque for USA-made instruments and use the Epiphone brand which they acquired in 1957 for their licensed import and budget Les Pauls.

The guitars fall into several distinct groupings:

■ Late prototypes and early production
From 1952–7 the Les Paul underwent quite radical refinement involving fundamental changes to the neck pitch, bridge assembly and type of pickup.

■ The golden age 1958–60
The above refinements led to an unprecedented golden age producing the rarest and most coveted of electric solid-body guitars. A 'burst from this Les Paul era is essentially the Stradivarius of electric guitars.

■ '70s and '80s reissues
The accuracy of these reissues is very controversial and several key elements of the Les Paul often seemed to be lacking, though plenty of good instruments were made.

■ The '90s and the 21st century 'Custom, Art & Historic' reissues and revised 'Stock' production
Gibson has latterly taken immense pride in researching

102

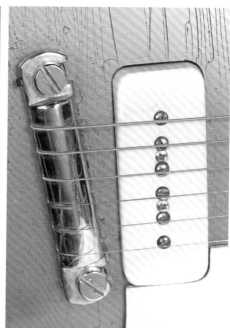

and developing accurate reproductions of its most classic instruments. These include slightly distressed 'relic' versions of the 'burst and Goldtops.

■ Parallel production USA Epiphones

For several years Epiphone continued USA production of classic Gibson-like guitars, usually with distinctive differences such as mini humbuckers. These are rare collectors' items.

■ Budget Epiphones

Since 1989 the Epiphone marque has appeared on a range of instruments manufactured in the Far East. Though variable in quality a good one makes a very workmanlike instrument and is the ideal look-alike for the wannabe. These are well worth

attention – perhaps upgrading the electronics and properly set up to create a professional instrument. Les Paul himself sincerely endorses these instruments.

■ Futuristic new models

The 'Digital' and 'Robot' are the most prominent of these, but 'green' guitars made of sustainable woods and lightweight 'female' Les Pauls such as the Vixen and Goddess appeal to a new audience. The latest guitar features 'slot in' pickups – the 'push tone'.

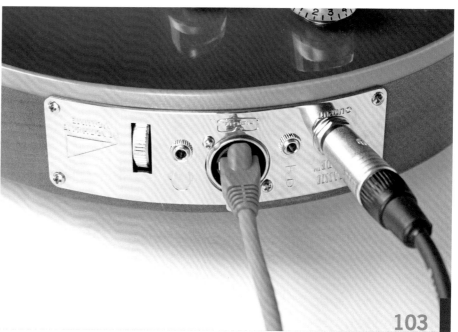

Custom Shop 'Regular' Quilt Top '59 neck

Serial No. 9 7858

Made in Nashville, Tennessee, in 2007, this guitar represents an example of the current Custom USA 'Regular', the 'Standard' designation not being assigned until 1960. These are offered with a variety of 'flame' effects to their glorious maple tops. This particular Quilt Top has an almost three-dimensional appearance, the maple having been specially selected and custom-sawn to enhance the once accidental beauty of exposed grain.

An original '59 would be the most expensive vintage guitar available – *if* they were available! So this attempt by the Gibson Custom Shop to provide an affordable alternative will be welcomed by many. I have never seen a real '59 with a 'quilt' top, but if there is one it may look like this. This guitar, however, is 'as new' and it will be interesting to see how it fades and mellows with time.

The neck has the chunky '59 profile, which you like or loath depending most probably on your hand size.

General description

■ The volume and tone knobs are the vintage type gold witches' hats, 'back painted' as on the vintage guitars.

■ The three-way switch has the graphics 'rhythm & treble' and has an appropriate new-minted appearance except for the switch cover, which is tastefully aged.

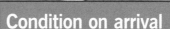

■ The pickup covers are nickel-plated in '50s style, though 'as new' and as bright as chromium.

■ The fingerboard is a raised thin-bound rosewood with a pronounced attractive grain.

■ The guitar is a relatively light 8.5lb (3.9kg), a nice concession and likely achieved through a careful choice of timber. This is the light end of comparative 'vintage' weights, the heaviest recorded 'burst being 9lb 11.4oz (4.4kg)! The body has the vintage sandwich of maple and mahogany, the bottom mahogany layer being one *solid* piece of timber.

■ Bridge

This is of the zinc alloy 'Tune-O-Matic' type ABR-1, but is slightly more substantial, less eccentric and probably better engineered than the hand-built originals. It retains the original height adjusting thumbscrews. The string length adjustment requires a conventional straight-slot 4.5mm screwdriver accessed from the pickup side. The bridge has '50s-type nickel-plated brass saddles and has a 'modern' saddle retaining spring. The stop bar is weight-reducing aluminium as found on the original '59 guitar and is a featherweight 35g.

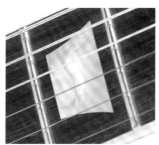

■ The fully bound fingerboard is of dark rosewood with 'pearl' trapezoid block inlays. The fingerboard radius is a traditional 12in, which in the factory set-up is not currently mirrored at the bridge.

■ The truss rod is accessed at the headstock, requiring a '1' point Phillips to remove the truss rod shield, which, historically correct, doesn't have a 'Standard' logo. The truss rod requires an 8mm socket wrench for any adjustment. The frets are a substantial 2.69mm gauge.

Condition on arrival

This new guitar is supplied with a plush-lined brown 'vintage' case with gilt fittings and a certificate of authenticity from the Gibson Custom and Historic Division.

■ Body

The body is approximately 5cm thick at the edge binding and 6cm at the highest point of the top carving – similar to the classic vintage guitars which naturally varied as a result of hand sanding. Some vintage Les Pauls are up to .5cm thicker! The vintage correct 'thin' binding is consistently world class and has a pleasant pre-aged appearance.

■ Neck

The neck profile is of a chunky rounded '59 profile with a fairly constant depth of approximately 22mm. It seems to be one piece with two small laminate wings to shape the headstock, the '70s volute at the 'weak' headstock junction is naturally omitted. The peghead pitch is a useful but slightly eccentric 16°, consistent with '50s hand-made tolerances.

■ The nut is a piece of white plastic which needs a little adjustment – the strings are binding in the slots, causing the intonation to drift. A little lubrication is all that's required.

■ The machine heads are vintage type 'single ring' late '50s Kluson look-alikes with green-tinged 'tulip' pegs.

■ The headstock has the distinctive small late '50s profile with a 'separated dot' Gibson logo.

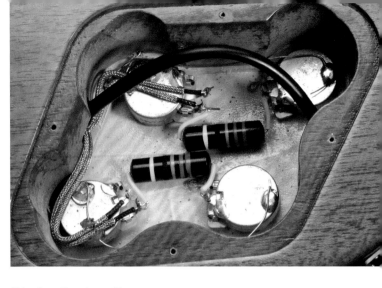

Specific routine maintenance

First check the neck relief with your feeler gauges. The neck should be fairly flat – perhaps .015 relief at the 7th fret given .012in at the 1st fret first string. If the neck does need adjustment, the 'Regular' requires either a suitable socket wrench or the supplied 8mm specialist wrench/screwdriver combo.

Follow the Vintage Les Paul set-up guide (see page 35) for any bridge height and intonation adjustments.

A factor worth considering is the string angle between the Tune-O-Matic bridge and the stop tailpiece. Ideally this should be a steep slope to give a good string purchase at the bridge. However, at too steep an angle the strings can snag on the back of the Tune-O-Matic. This may cause premature string breakage as well as unpredictable string slippage. This specific guitar has been well set up with a good .037 clearance at the 6th string.

The strings on this guitar are vintage reissue .010–.046, lighter than would have been available in '59 but consistent with modern requirements. When changing strings it's worth checking the machine-head fixing screws, which tend to work loose. This requires a '1' point Phillips. Do not over-tighten them – just enough to stop the machine head moving in normal use.

Whilst you have the tools out it's worth tightening the output jack retainer. This tends to work loose, causing crackles and intermittent output. Tightening entails removing the square plastic jack socket panel using a '1' point Phillips and getting a grip on the jack socket itself as you tighten the exterior nut with a ½in socket spanner. The quality of the screws used on these USA guitars is much higher and this makes maintenance much easier.

The guitar is supplied without a scratchplate, and who would want to hide such an interesting wood grain!

The strap buttons are worth checking for secure fitting. If a '1' point Phillips screwdriver can't secure the screw then consider an improvised rawlplug made from a spent matchstick and a little superglue.

The frets are nicely polished and feel good as supplied. If they ever need a polish then a simple cardboard template and some light abrasive such as Planet Waves fret-polishing paper will do the trick. Similarly the rosewood may benefit from a little lemon oil.

'Under the hood'

Removing the rear access panel using the usual '1' point Phillips screwdriver reveals a very clean rout, and the huge period correct 'bumble bee' capacitors. During these inspections an aerosol lid can make a useful 'screw keep', avoiding accidental losses.

■ The wiring is very clean, with four small 500K pots and two .02mF capacitors routed to a three-way switch. All the wiring is heavily screened with a braided exterior. The pots are mounted direct to the wood. The black backing plates for the control cavities are an authentic vintage touch.

■ If loose, the volume and tone pots require a wrapped-round duster to safely remove the push-fit knob, and then a 0.5in socket spanner for removal or adjustment of the pot itself. Take care not to impale your fingers on the period-correct metal indicator flange.

■ The three-way switch really needs a specialist tool for tightening and replacement – the plastic type protects the metal plating from damage (see photo below left).

■ If required, replacing the three-way switch is done via another rear pane (see 'Replacing a three-way selector', page 44). A modern 'rounded end' paperclip is a useful gizmo for removing these rear panels, as they're often a tight fit even when unscrewed. The rounded end avoids any potential scratching. All the panels are authentic black plastic with a gloss finish.

■ The pickup pole pieces in their custom cases require a 4mm straight-slot screwdriver for adjusting their height in relation to the strings.

■ If for any reason you're removing *all* the strings then an elastic band prevents the loose stop bar and possibly the Tune-O-Matic falling off and doing damage to the precious quilt top.

■ Revealed by removing the four Phillips '1' point screws, the 'Regular' has USA PAF humbucking pickups. These are designated 'BB#1 wound by PS' and have a PAF designation label presumably referring to the original Seth Lover specification. Be aware,

however, that the specific windings are more likely the modern BurstBucker specification. If the pickups have been wax dipped there is no sloppy excess revealed around the case. Access to the fragile coils is sensibly denied by a soldered seal.

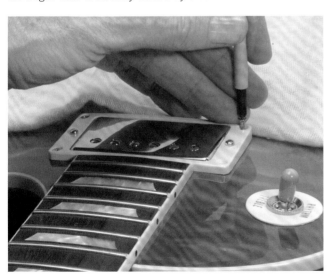

Removing the metal 'cans' or cases is NOT recommended. Though this might look cool, it exposes the pickups to environmental damage, will permit some induced hum and will only make the pickups more treble-biased (due to stray capacitance) – the sound of a Les Paul is a warmer tone best left alone. If you want the 'cool' bare pickup look this is easily achieved by buying a set of open case pickups from Seymour Duncan or similar. The overall pickup height adjustment is effected by two 4mm head straight-slot screws attached to a rear metal bracket. 'Springing' is achieved by two substantial springs. Take care when reseating humbuckers to ensure their correct orientation. In the case of the neck pickup this means putting the adjustable pole pieces nearest to the fingerboard.

■ The neck pickup cavity does reveal the Les Paul signature 'long tenon'. On the original guitars this contributes to the strength of the neck join and the rigidity of the guitar, a key factor in the Les Paul sound. There is also substantial weight-relieving routing forming the wiring cavities. The bridge pickup is designated '#2 wound by PS'. Note for authenticity all the pickup fixing screws are the same length – in this respect modern improvements are not allowed!

Signed off

This guitar does require a little setting up. The nut could be filed a little lower. The Tune-O-Matic could also come down a little and the saddles could be usefully filed to mirror the fingerboard radius. But these are largely 'customer taste' issues wisely left to the owner's guitar tech.

This is a classic Les Paul and when wound up delivers something very like the classic 'burst sound. The hardware is all present and correct; the Peter Green 'software' is not yet available so it's back to the woodshed.

Gibson Les Paul
'Standard' '60s neck

Serial No. 25160465

Made in Nashville, Tennessee, in 2006, this guitar represents a good example of the current USA 'Standard'. These often have an attractive 'flame' effect to their maple tops. This particular guitar is a bit of a hybrid, finished in Honeyburst, the 'faded' version of what in 1960 at last became the Les Paul 'Standard'. It is lacquered traditionally, which may perhaps fade to the lemon-drop 'burst effect of the 1950s! I say *may* because by 1960 the sunburst lacquers had been adjusted to not fade. The neck, however, has the popular thin 1960 profile. The guitar bears a close affinity to Serial No 9 2229, a genuine Honeyburst '59. It has USA-made BurstBuckers with Alnico V magnets.

General description

■ The volume and tone knobs are the vintage-type gold witches' hats, 'back painted' as on the vintage guitars.

■ The three-way switch has the graphics 'rhythm & treble' and has an appropriate new minted appearance.

■ The pickup covers are nickel-plated in '50s style, though 'as new' and as bright as chromium.

108

■ The fingerboard is a raised bound rosewood with a pronounced attractive grain.

■ The guitar is a hefty 9.5lb (4.3kg), a real Les Paul shoulder-breaker (Lester told me he would be remembered 'for services to orthopaedic medicine'), the weight you need, however, for the kind of rigidity that produces the distinctive character of the Les Paul sound – Lester's 'railway track with strings'. This is at the heavy end of vintage weights. The body has the vintage sandwich of maple and mahogany, the bottom mahogany layer being one *solid* piece of timber.

■ Bridge

The newer-type zinc alloy Tune-O-Matic is slightly more substantial, less eccentric and better engineered than the hand-built originals and has the usual thumbscrews for height adjustment. The string length adjustment requires a conventional straight-slot 4.5mm screwdriver accessed from the tailpiece side. The bridge has '50s-type nickel-plated saddles and lacks a 'modern' retaining spring. An elastic band will suffice for this role when removing all the strings. As it happens the modern accurate engineering means the bridge is quite snug on the screw posts and is unlikely to fall off. It is designated PW. The stop bar is *not* weight-reducing aluminium as found on the original '60s guitar and weighs a substantial 85g.

■ Body

Approximately 50mm thick at the edge binding and 60mm at the highest point of the top carving – similar to the classic vintage guitars, which naturally varied as a result of hand sanding. Some vintage Les Pauls are up to 5mm thicker! The binding is consistently world class.

■ Neck

The profile follows a typical 'slimmer' 1960 profile with a fairly constant depth. The neck appears to be three-piece laminate, which is a good choice for stability and tonally favourable rigidity. It has a narrow '60s heel and no clumsy volute at the 'weak' headstock junction. The peghead pitch is a useful 17°. However, Les Paul himself told me he feels this pitch angle is not overly critical.

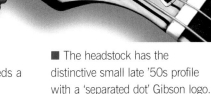

■ The nut is a piece of white plastic which needs a little adjustment.

■ The machine heads are vintage type 'single ring' late '50s early 1960 Kluson look-alikes with green-tinged 'tulip' pegs.

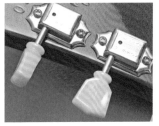

■ The truss rod is accessed at the headstock, requiring a '1' point Phillips to remove the truss rod shield, which, historically correct, doesn't have a 'Standard' logo. The truss rod requires an 8mm socket wrench or Gibson's own supplied tool for any adjustment. The frets are the narrow 2.38mm gauge found on many early Les Pauls.

■ The headstock has the distinctive small late '50s profile with a 'separated dot' Gibson logo.

■ The fully bound fingerboard is of a dark rosewood with 'pearl' trapezoid block inlays. The fingerboard radius is a traditional 12in.

Condition on arrival

This new guitar is supplied with a plush-lined black reptile-effect case, proudly labelled 'Made in Canada'.

Specific routine maintenance

First check the neck relief with your feeler gauges. The neck should be fairly flat – perhaps .015 relief at the 7th fret given .012in at the 1st fret first string. If the neck does need adjustment, the 'Standard' requires an 8mm socket wrench.

Follow the Vintage Les Paul set-up guide (*page 35*) for any bridge height and intonation adjustments.

A factor worth considering is the string angle between the Tune-O-Matic bridge and the stop tailpiece. Ideally this should be a steep slope to give a good string purchase at the bridge. However, at too steep an angle the strings can snag on the back of the Tune-O-Matic. This may cause premature string breakage as well as unpredictable string slippage. This specific guitar has been well set up with a good .008mm clearance on the 6th string.

The strings on this guitar are Brite Wires .010–.046, a common choice for this shorter scale guitar. When changing strings it's worth checking the machine-head fixing screws, which tend to work loose. This requires a '1' point Phillips. Do not over-tighten them – just enough to stop the machine head moving in normal use.

Whilst you have the tools out it's worth tightening the output jack retainer. This tends to work loose, causing crackles and intermittent output. Tightening entails removing the square plastic jack socket panel using a '1' point Phillips and getting a grip on the jack socket itself as you tighten the exterior nut with a ½in socket spanner. It may seem a small point but the quality of the screws used on these USA guitars is much higher and this makes maintenance so much easier.

The guitar is supplied with a scratchplate and screws, but note how much better the guitar looks without the afterthought rocket tailfin scratchplate.

The strap buttons are worth checking for secure fitting. If a '1' point Phillips screwdriver can't secure the screw then consider an improvised rawlplug made from a spent matchstick and a little superglue.

If, as in this case, the frets need a little polish then a simple cardboard template and some light abrasive such as Planet Waves fret polishing paper will do the trick. Similarly the rosewood may benefit from a little lemon oil.

'Under the hood'

Removing the rear access panel using the usual '1' point Phillips screwdriver reveals a very clean rout, and a screening plate for attaching the Gibson pots. Note that no attempt has been made to use authentic 'antique alike' components on this 21st-century guitar. However, any 1930s radio repair man would be very at home with these parts. During these inspections an aerosol lid can make a useful 'screw keep', avoiding accidental losses.

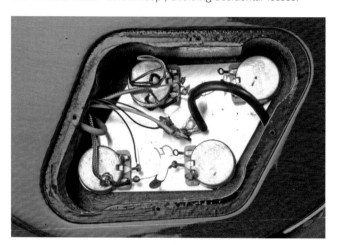

■ The wiring is very clean with four small modern 500K pots and two .02mF capacitors routed to a three-way switch. All the wire is modern PVC-covered. The pots are mounted to a screening plate and all the wiring is screened using individually earthed looms. The black backing plates for the control cavities are an authentic vintage touch.

■ If loose, the volume and tone pots require a wrapped-round duster to safely remove the push-fit knob and then a 0.5in socket spanner for removal or adjustment of the pot itself.

■ The three-way switch really needs a specialist tool for tightening and replacement – the plastic type protects the metal plating from damage.

■ If required, replacing the three-way switch is done via another rear pane (see 'Replacing a three-way selector', page 44). A modern 'rounded end' paperclip is a useful gizmo for removing these rear panels, as they're often a tight fit even when unscrewed. The rounded end avoids any potential scratching.

■ The Gibson BurstBucker-type pickups in their custom cases require a 4mm straight-slot screwdriver for adjusting their height in relation to the strings.

■ If for any reason you're removing *all* the strings then an elastic band prevents the loose stop bar falling off and doing damage.

■ Revealed by removing the four Phillips '1' point screws, the 'Standard' has USA BurstBucker humbucking pickups. These are designated 'No 1 ALV wound by PS' and have a PAF

designation which presumably refers to the BurstBucker specification, not Seth Lover's. If the pickups have been wax dipped there is no sloppy excess revealed around the case. Access to the fragile coils is sensibly denied by a soldered seal.

Removing the metal 'cans' or cases is NOT recommended. Though this might look cool it exposes the pickups to environmental damage, will permit some induced hum and will only make the pickups more treble-biased (due to stray capacitance) – the sound of a Les Paul is a warmer tone best left alone. If you want the 'cool' bare pickup look this is easily achieved by buying a set of open case pickups from Seymour Duncan or similar.

The overall pickup height adjustment is effected by two 4mm

straight slot screws attached to a rear metal bracket. 'Springing' is achieved by two substantial springs. The individual pickup pole adjustment requires a 4.5mm straight-slot screwdriver. Take care when reseating humbuckers to ensure their correct orientation. In the case of the neck pickup this means putting the adjustable pole pieces nearest to the fingerboard.

■ The neck pickup cavity reveals the *absence* of the Les Paul signature 'long tenon'. On the original guitars this contributes to the strength of the neck join and the rigidity of the guitar – a key factor in the Les Paul sound. There is, however, some weight-relieving routing forming the wiring cavities. The bridge pickup is designated 'No 2ALV wound by PS'. When replacing the bridge pickup note the modern 'longer screws at the back, shorter screws at the front' arrangement.

Signed off

The 'Standard' required little setting up. The nut could be filed a little lower and the Tune-O-Matic could also come down a little, but this is all to be expected in a factory-finished guitar. This is a classic Les Paul and when wound up delivers something very like the classic 'burst sound – perhaps a little hotter due to the modern BurstBuckers.

Epiphone 'Standard' plus made in China

Made in 2006, this guitar represents a typical example of the Epiphone 'Standard'. These now have a 'plus' top veneer featuring an attractive 'flame' effect. This particular guitar is finished in Cherry Sunburst, the original colour of what was in 1958 the Les Paul 'Regular'. Ironically the guitar is finished with modern lacquers which will not fade to the coveted faded 'burst effect of the 1950s! Pre-faded versions are available, however.

Serial No. DW05110616

It has factory-fitted Epiphone USA-designed humbuckers with alnico magnets, which are double vacuum waxed with enamel wire. These sound pretty good but on page 80 we experiment with Seymour Duncan replacements – a common upgrade for this guitar.

General description

■ The volume and tone knobs are the vintage-type gold witches' hats, but moulded gold plastic, not 'back painted' as on the vintage guitars.

■ The three-way switch has the graphics 'rhythm & treble' and has an appropriate new minted appearance.

■ The pickup covers are chromium plated, as are almost all the metal parts.

■ The fingerboard is raised bound rosewood.

■ At 7.75lb (3.5kg) the guitar is comfortably light for a Les Paul and may have some weight-reducing cavities. The body appears to be the vintage sandwich of maple and mahogany – however, the low weight points to alder with a thin veneer of mahogany and maple. The thick cherry-coloured finish cannot disguise the fact that the bottom 'mahogany' layer is in fact made up of at least three separate pieces of timber. This is no crime, especially in an economy guitar – we should remember that the first Goldtops often had three-piece carved tops – and in the climate of the early 21st century, the recycling of what are probably offcuts is indeed a laudable endeavour. The laminate nature of all Les Pauls is, in fact, a major contributor to the guitar's famous rigidity – the 'railway track' principle Lester Polfus describes in the intro to this book. Alder is a great tonewood which produces a brighter sound than mahogany.

■ Bridge

Of the Tune-O-Matic type with the usual thumbscrews for height adjustment and convenient Epiphone top screws – this bridge is on separate posts *not* set directly into the table.

■ The string length adjustment requires a conventional straight-slot 4.5mm screwdriver accessed from the pickup side. The bridge has '50s-type metal saddles but with a 'modern' retaining spring.

■ Body

Approximately 45mm thick at the edge binding and 55mm at the highest point of the top carving, slightly thinner than some vintage guitars. Some of the binding is a little low-budget. The apparent 'flamed' top is a very thin veneer, as is common on these budget guitars, but is very convincing.

■ Neck

Profile follows a typical slimmer, almost 1960 profile with a fairly constant depth. It seems one piece and is too heavily stained for wood identification. It has a narrow '60s heel.

■ The fully bound fingerboard is of a dark rosewood with plastic trapezoid block inlays. The fingerboard radius is a 'blues friendly' 14in – unusual for a Les Paul, which is more often 12in.

■ The truss rod is accessed at the headstock, requiring a '1' point Phillips to remove the truss rod shield with its distinctive 'Les Paul Standard' logo and a 4mm Allen wrench for any adjustment. The frets are the 2.78mm/.109in gauge found on many later Les Pauls.

■ The supplied nut is a piece of plastic which needs some adjustment – *see page 88* for a modification to bone.

■ The machine heads are good modern chrome Grovers with 'Ace of Clubs' tuning pegs.

■ The headstock has one of the distinctive Epiphone shapes first established in the 1930s.

■ The headstock angle is approx 17°, unusual for an Epiphone but very welcome, giving a good downward pressure at the nut – important for tone and string stability.

Specific routine maintenance

First check the neck relief with your feeler gauges. The neck should be fairly flat – perhaps .015 relief at the 7th fret given .012in at the 1st fret first string. If the neck does need adjustment, the 'Standard' requires the supplied 4mm wrench.

Follow the Vintage Les Paul set-up guide (*page 35*) for any bridge height and intonation adjustments.

A factor worth considering is the string angle between the Tune-O-Matic bridge and the stop tailpiece. Ideally this should be a steep slope to give a good string purchase at the bridge.

However, at too steep an angle the strings can snag on the back of the Tune-O-Matic, which may cause premature string breakage as well as unpredictable string slippage. This specific guitar has been well set up with a good clearance.

The strings are .010–.046, a common choice for this shorter scale guitar. When changing strings it's worth checking the machine-head fixing screws, which tend to work loose. This requires a '1' point Phillips. Do not over-tighten them – just enough to stop the machine head moving in normal use. The Grovers also have tension screws for the machine heads, which should be loosened for string changes using a '1' point Phillips and re-tensioned once the guitar is at pitch.

Whilst you have the tools out it's worth tightening the output jack retainer. This tends to work loose, causing crackles and intermittent output. Tightening entails removing the square plastic jack socket panel using a '1' point Phillips and getting a grip on the 12mm rear jack socket nut as you tighten the exterior nut with a 12mm socket spanner.

The scratchplate retaining bracket is best tightened OFF the guitar, as the rear nut is otherwise difficult to adjust without damage to the guitar top. Removing the scratchplate itself

requires a '1' point Phillips screwdriver, and for tightening the rear retaining nut a 7mm socket spanner. Note how much better the guitar looks without the 'afterthought' scratchplate.

The strap buttons are worth checking for secure fitting. If a '1' point Phillips screwdriver can't secure the screw then consider an improvised rawlplug made from a spent matchstick and a little superglue.

Under the hood

Removing the rear access panel using the usual '1' point Phillips screwdriver reveals a fairly clean rout, a little tatty around one of the pots, but the minimum of wood has been removed. During these inspections an aerosol lid can make a useful 'screw keep', avoiding accidental losses.

■ The wiring is competent, with four small modern 500K pots and .02mF capacitors routed to a three-way switch. All the wire is modern PVC-covered. The pots are roughly mounted to bare or painted wood and all the wiring is

screened using an earthed
loom. A nice touch is the
modern wiring connector,
which may make things easier
and convenient should you
wish to change pickups. The
cream backing plates for the
control cavities are a nice
touch – a change from the
traditional black.

■ Revealed by removing
the four Phillips '1' point
screws, the 'Standard' has
USA-designed Epiphone
humbucking pickups. These
are designated '57 CH (G)
Dot neck/bridge LP and bridge
HOTCH (G) BHC'. '57' may
refer to the PAF spec and BH to
BurstBucker. The pickups have
been twice wax dipped – a
measure which reduces any tendency to high-frequency
audio feedback. Access to the fragile coils is sensibly denied by
a soldered seal.

■ If loose, the volume and
tone pots require a wrapped-
round duster to safely remove
the push-fit knob and then an
11mm/0.5in socket spanner
for removal or adjustment of
the pot itself.

Removing the metal 'cans' or cases is NOT recommended.
Though this might look cool it exposes the pickups to environmental
damage, will permit some induced hum and will only make the
pickups more treble-biased (due to stray capacitance) – the sound
of a Les Paul is a warmer tone best left alone. If you want the 'cool'
bare pickup look this is easily achieved by buying a set of open case
pickups from Seymour Duncan or similar.

■ The three-way switch really needs a specialist tool for
tightening and replacement – the plastic type protects the metal
plating from damage.

The overall pickup height adjustment is effected by two Phillips '1'
screws attached to a rear metal plate. 'Springing' is achieved by two
substantial springs. The individual pickup pole adjustment requires a
4mm straight-slot screwdriver. Take care when reseating humbuckers
to ensure their correct orientation. In the case of the neck pickup this
means putting the adjustable pole pieces nearest to the fingerboard.

■ If required, replacing the cheap but serviceable three-way
switch is done via another rear pane (see 'Replacing a three-
way selector', page 44). A modern 'rounded end' paperclip is a
useful gizmo for removing these rear panels, as they are often
a tight fit even when unscrewed. The rounded end avoids any
potential scratching. All the panels are this complementary
cream plastic with a textured finish.

■ The neck pickup cavity reveals the *absence* of the Les Paul
signature 'long tenon'. On the 'full price' guitars this contributes
to the strength of the neck join and the rigidity of the guitar – a
key factor in the Les Paul sound. Also revealed are some of the
weight-relieving cavities often found on modern guitars – welcome
in some ways, but also a factor in moving away from the classic
Les Paul.

■ The full-size Epiphone humbucker-type pickups in their
custom cases require a '1' point Phillips screwdriver for
adjusting their height in relation to the strings.

■ The bridge pickup is designated 'HOTCH (G) LP bridge BHC'.

Signed off

The Epiphone 'Standard' required substantial setting up. Some of the
frets were a little proud, the nut could be filed a little lower, and the
Tune-O-Matic could come down a little, but this is all to be expected
in a factory-finished economy guitar.

■ If for any reason you are removing *all* the strings then
an elastic band prevents the loose stop bar falling off and
doing damage.

This is a lot of Les Paul for the money and when wound up
delivers something very like the classic 'burst sound. Some people
have experienced problems with these guitars when wound up very
loud so please see page 80 for a suggested pickup swap.

Epiphone '56 Goldtop made in China

Made in 2007, this guitar is an affordable nod to the classic Goldtop as it finally came of age in 1956 with a stop tail bridge and Tune-O-Matic. It's equipped with a version of the single coil P90 pickups as used on the very first Les Pauls *(see 'Goldtop "Regular" made in 1953', page 130)*.

Serial No. EE070801479

General description

■ The volume and tone knobs are vintage-type gold witches' hats 'back painted' as on the vintage guitars.

■ The three-way switch has the graphics 'rhythm & treble' and has an appropriate new minted appearance.

■ The pickups are cream-coloured P90 'soapbars' in '50s style.

■ The fingerboard is raised bound rosewood with an attractive grain.

■ The guitar is a light 7.5lb (3.4kg) – a delight! This weight reduction is achieved by using lighter alder for the body mass with a mahogany veneer for the back. Alder is a great tone wood, and nobody needs orthopaedic problems.

■ Bridge

Of the newer Epiphone Tune-O-Matic type, this is slightly more substantial, less eccentric and better engineered than the hand-built originals, and has the usual thumbscrews for height adjustment as well as the convenient top-screw Epiphone adjustment. String-length adjustment requires a conventional straight-slot

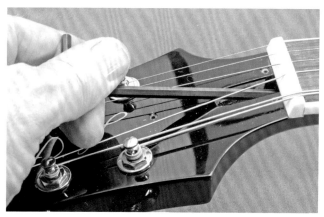

4.5mm screwdriver and is accessed from the pickup side. The bridge has chrome-plated saddles which are kept in place by a 'modern' retaining spring. The stop bar is *not* weight-reducing aluminium as found on the original '56 guitar but is not over heavy at 72g.

■ Body

Approximately 50mm thick at the edge binding and 55mm at the highest point of the top carving – slightly slimmer than the classic vintage guitars, which did vary, however, as a result of hand-sanding. The binding is the slim economy type.

■ Neck

The mahogany neck is a nice compromise, neither over-chunky '50s nor over-slim '60s. The peghead pitch is an unusual but correct 17°.

■ The fully bound fingerboard is rosewood with pearl-effect trapezoid block inlays. The fingerboard radius is a traditional 12in, and this is not quite yet reflected at the bridge.

■ The truss rod is accessed at the headstock, requiring a '1' point Phillips to remove the truss rod shield, which has the '56 Goldtop logo. The truss rod requires a 4mm Allen wrench for any adjustment. The frets are medium 2.74mm gauge.

■ The nut is a piece of white plastic which needs a little setting up.

■ The machine heads are modern fairly robust Grovers.

■ The headstock has the distinctive Epiphone profile with a tasteful pearl-effect logo.

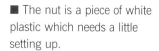

Condition on arrival

This new budget guitar arrived very crudely set up with a very high nut and raw unpolished frets. However, it won't need much attention to turn it into a fine instrument. The acoustic sound is bright and resonant and the Alnico V P90s deliver a classic sound.

Specific routine maintenance

First check the neck relief with your feeler gauges. The neck should be fairly flat – perhaps .015 relief at the 7th fret given .012in at the 1st fret first string. If the neck does need adjustment, the Goldtop requires a 4mm Allen wrench.

Follow the Epiphone Les Paul set-up guide (*page 35*) for any bridge height and intonation adjustments.

A factor worth considering is the string angle between the Tune-O-Matic bridge and the stop tailpiece. Ideally this should be a steep slope to give a good string purchase at the bridge. However, at too steep an angle the strings can snag on the back of the Tune-O-Matic, which may cause premature string breakage as well as unpredictable string slippage. This specific guitar needs some setting up.

The strings are .010–.046, a common choice for this shorter scale guitar. On new guitars it's worth checking the machine-head fixing screws, which tend to work loose due to early shrinkage. This requires a '1' point Phillips. Do not over-tighten them – just enough to stop the machine head moving in normal use.

You could usefully check the machine-head locking nuts, which similarly work loose, causing tuning instability. This requires a 10mm socket wrench.

Whilst you have the tools out it's worth tightening the output jack retainer. This tends to work loose, causing crackles and intermittent output. Tightening entails removing the square plastic jack socket panel using a '1' point Phillips and getting a grip on the jack socket itself as you tighten the exterior nut with a 12mm socket spanner.

The guitar is supplied with a scratchplate and the gold top looks just right with its '50s rocket tailfin in place.

The strap buttons are worth checking for secure fitting. If a '2' point Phillips screwdriver can't secure the screw then consider an improvised rawlplug made from a spent matchstick and a little superglue.

If, as in this case, the frets need a little polish then a simple cardboard template and some light abrasive such as Planet Waves fret polishing paper will do the trick. Similarly, the very dry rosewood will benefit from a *little* lemon oil.

Under the hood

Removing the rear access panel using the usual '1' point Phillips screwdriver reveals a rough and ready rout, with the small pots attached directly to the wood. During these inspections a discarded floss container can make a useful 'screw keep', avoiding accidental losses.

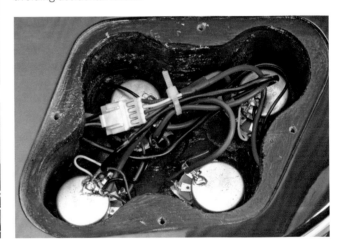

■ The wiring is adequate with four small modern 500K pots and two .02mF capacitors routed to a three-way switch. All the wire is modern PVC-covered and has a useful cable joint for maintenance. There is an intermittent concession to screening paint in the control cavity.

■ If loose, the volume and tone pots require a wrapped-round duster to safely remove the push-fit knob and then an 11mm socket spanner for removal or adjustment of the pot itself.

■ The small three-way switch really needs a specialist tool for tightening and replacement – a plastic tool protects the metal plating from damage (*page 110*).

■ If required, replacing the three-way switch with the larger Gibson professional type is done via another rear panel (*see 'Replacing a three-way selector', page 44*). A modern 'rounded end' paperclip is a useful gizmo for removing these rear panels, as they are often a tight fit even when unscrewed. The rounded end avoids any potential scratching. All the panels are cream plastic with a matt finish – the 'originals' would have been brown.

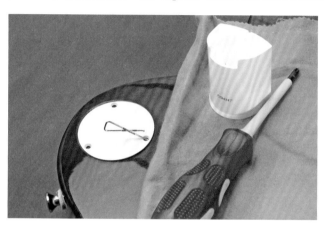

■ The P90-type pickups in their soap dish cases require a 'O' point Phillips screwdriver for adjusting their height in relation to the strings (*see note above right*).

■ If for any reason you are removing *all* the strings then an elastic band prevents the loose stop bar falling off and doing damage. However, this guitar incorporates a fairly recent Epiphone innovation: a pair of simple spring clips which hold the bar in place without string tension – very effective!

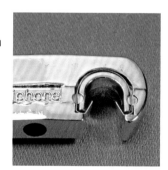

■ It's worth checking the stop bar posts are secure as these can affect the guitar's tone. This requires a beefy 12mm/0.5in straight-slot screwdriver and a little tape to protect the chrome.

■ Revealed by removing the two huge 36mm Phillips 'O' point screws, the Goldtop has single coil P90 pickups. These are designated 'Neck Pickups BHC' and are RoHS Directive compliant.* The pickup height engineering is simply the strain of the two wood screws against some foam rubber padding. Do not over-tighten these – there are hundreds of Goldtops out there with fractured soap dishes.

■ Note the scratchplate has had to be unscrewed to free the pickup. Some surplus wax suggests the pickups are wax dipped (sometimes an effective cure for feedback problems with P90s). The coil itself is easily loosened from its plastic soap dish.

■ Individual pickup pole adjustment requires a 4mm straight-slot screwdriver. This is best done with the strings in place – getting too close to a string may cause magnetic interference with its natural excursion. This causes 'beats' and consequent tuning problems.

■ The neck pickup cavity reveals the *absence* of the Les Paul signature 'long tenon' – on the original guitars this contributes to the strength of the neck join and the rigidity of the guitar, thought by some to be a key factor in the Les Paul sound. There is, however, substantial weight-relieving routing forming the wiring cavities. The bridge pickup is designated 'Bridge Pickups BHC' and is also RoHC compliant.

Signed off

The Goldtop required a little setting up. The nut could be filed a little lower and the Tune-O-Matic could also come down a little, but this is all to be expected in a factory-finished guitar. The frets need a dress and polish.

This is a working replica of the first classic incarnation of the Les Paul guitar and when wound up delivers something very like the classic P90 sound – a lot of guitar for the money. It performed with a certain style in the presence of it's '53 relative.

*RoHS stands for 'the restriction of the use of certain hazardous substances in electrical and electronic equipment'. This Directive bans the placing on the EU market of new electrical and electronic equipment containing more than agreed levels of lead, cadmium, mercury, hexavalent chromium, polybrominated biphenyl (PBB) and polybrominated diphenyl ether (PBDE) flame retardants.

USA-made 'Custom, Art & Historic Division' LPB 7 Vintage Reissue

Serial No. 711755

Made in 2001, this guitar represents a typical example of the current Gibson reissues of their golden age Les Pauls. It has been built to closely resemble a guitar produced in 1957 and originally had an 'as new' finish and was supplied in an authentic late '50s plush-lined shaped case. Two-pickup 'Customs' are very rare and were only originally made as customer special orders, so this is an unusual guitar.

General description

Superficially this may look like any other 'Black Beauty', However, a closer look reveals close attention to authentic 1957 detail as well as a few anachronistic anomalies.

■ The volume and tone knobs are the late '50s type still employed on some guitars in 2008.

■ The three-way switch has the graphics 'rhythm & treble' and has a tasteful artificially aged golden yellow colour to the plastic knob.

■ The pickup covers are 'gold'-plated, as are almost all the metal parts.

■ The fingerboard is a raised bound ebony type.

■ The body is solid mahogany, even the strikingly glossy carved top – which is a controversial variant. Ironically Les Paul had originally intended that the Goldtop should be solid mahogany and that the 'luxury' black guitars he preferred should have the sustain-enhancing maple top. Obviously the laminate maple top is a more labour intensive and therefore more expensive manufacturing option. Note the guitar is bound front *and* back.

■ Bridge

Of the original ABR-1 Tune-O-Matic type with the usual thumbscrews for height adjustment. The string length adjustment requires a conventional straight-slot 5mm screwdriver. Despite the ABR1 designation the bridge has the 'modern' (1962) type retaining spring for the bridge saddles, unusually combined with '50s-type metal saddles.

■ Body

The guitar is a heavy 9lb (4.5kg), but nevertheless slightly lighter than our maple-top reissue. The body thickness is approximately 50mm at the edge binding and 55mm at the highest point of the top carving.

■ Neck

Follows a typical 'half-round' 1957 profile with a fairly constant depth, 25mm at the 1st fret only increasing to 27mm near the heel – chunky or substantial depending on your point of view.

■ The fully bound fingerboard is high-quality ebony with real mother of pearl oblong block inlays. The fingerboard radius is a flat 12in.

■ The truss rod is accessed at the headstock, requiring a '0' point Phillips to remove the truss rod shield and a Gibson-supplied 8mm/0.3in wrench for any adjustment. The frets are 2.34mm/.092in gauge and show some very slight wear.

■ The nut is a well cut piece of bone-like plastic.

■ The machine heads are substantial 'gold'-plated Grovers. This is a tiny anachronism as these Grovers were not originally fitted until '58.

Condition on arrival

The guitar has been well played in over the last few years and this shows up as faint scratches on the black nitro-cellulose finish. The owner has recently changed the strings up a gauge to '10s'. This has resulted in a slight increase in neck relief. Also the Tune-O-Matic bridge is set slightly high and needs a little intonation adjustment. The stop tail is screwed down hard to the body, giving a very steep break angle for the strings at the bridge.

Specific routine maintenance

First check the neck relief with your feeler gauges. The neck should be fairly flat – perhaps .015in relief at the 7th fret given .012in at the 1st fret first string. If the neck does need adjustment, as here, the '57 requires a specialist 8mm wrench.

Follow the Vintage Les Paul set-up guide (*page 35*) for any bridge height and intonation adjustments.

A factor worth considering is the string angle between the Tune-O-Matic bridge and the stop tailpiece. Ideally this should be a steep slope to give a good string purchase at the bridge. However, at too steep an angle the strings can snag on the back of the Tune-O-Matic, which may cause premature string breakage as well as unpredictable string slippage. This specific guitar has exactly that problem. Simply raising the stop bar slightly with a 12mm straight-slot screwdriver resolved the issue. Interestingly this also improved the sound and 'feel' of the guitar.

The strings on this guitar are .010–.046 Ernie Balls. When changing strings, it's worth checking the machine-head fixing screws, which tend to work loose. On the '57 this requires a '1' point Phillips. Do not over-tighten them – just enough to stop the machine-head moving in normal use.

Also loosen the machine-head tension screws for string changing and restore the tension once the strings are at pitch – do not over-tighten! On this guitar you'll need a '1' point Phillips screwdriver.

Whilst you have the tools out it's worth tightening the output jack retainer. This tends to work loose, causing crackles and intermittent output. Tightening entails removing the square jack socket using a '1' point Phillips and getting a grip on the jack retainer itself as you tighten the bolt with a 13mm/0.5in socket spanner.

The scratchplate retaining bracket is best tightened OFF the guitar, as the rear nut is otherwise difficult to adjust without damage to the guitar top. Removing the scratchplate itself

requires a '1' point Phillips screwdriver, and for tightening the rear nut a 5/16in socket spanner.

The guitar has a retro-fitted 'strap lock', but despite the security this affords, the strap lock is only as secure as its fittings. If a '1' point Phillips screwdriver can't secure the screw, then consider an improvised rawlplug made from a spent matchstick and a little superglue.

Under the hood

Removing the rear access panel using the usual '1' point Phillips screwdriver reveals a clean rout. The minimum of wood has been removed. During these inspections an aerosol lid can make a useful 'screw keep', avoiding accidental losses.

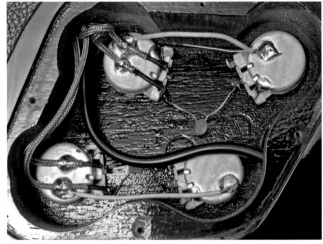

■ The wiring is impeccable with four classic 500K pots and .02 mF capacitors routed to a three-way switch. All the wire is modern PVC-covered.

■ There is no electrical screening in the control compartment.

■ If loose, the volume and tone pots require a wrapped-round duster to safely remove the push-fit knob and then a 0.5in socket spanner for removal or adjustment of the pot itself.

■ The three-way switch really needs a specialist tool for tightening and replacement – the shown plastic type protects the gold plating from damage. However, the plastic is easily stripped if the nut is too tight!

■ Replacing the three-way switch if required is done via another rear panel (*see 'Replacing a three-way selector', page 44*).

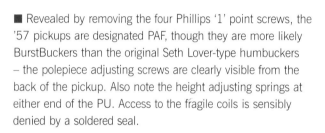

■ The heavily wound PAF-type pickups in their '57 cases require a '1' point Phillips screwdriver for adjusting their height in relation to the strings.

■ Revealed by removing the four Phillips '1' point screws, the '57 pickups are designated PAF, though they are more likely BurstBuckers than the original Seth Lover-type humbuckers – the polepiece adjusting screws are clearly visible from the back of the pickup. Also note the height adjusting springs at either end of the PU. Access to the fragile coils is sensibly denied by a soldered seal.

■ The neck pickup cavity reveals the important neck joint 'long tenon' adding rigidity to the original Les Paul specification.

Signed off

The 'Custom' required a little adjustment. The neck relief problem was most likely attributable to the change of string gauge, as was the small adjustment to the intonation. As found, the truss rod actually displayed no tension at all, which is probably due to a little wood shrinkage.

As it stands the 'Custom' is not truly a 'fretless wonder' and would need a little fret dressing and finishing to live up to that accolade. It is, however, a fine guitar which when turned up to 11 delivers all the expected 'Spinal Tap'.

USA-made
HD 6X Pro

Serial No. 033260313

Made in Nashville, Tennessee, in 2007, this guitar marks a bold recent venture by Gibson – the 'Digital' Les Paul.

Guitar players tend to stick to tried and trusted guitars and Gibson have taken this on board. They offer everything we covet in a traditional Les Paul and then go 'one more' by offering that in electric blue with a sprinkling of creative possibility.

The heart of the new guitar is the additional HEX pickup located just in front of the Tune-O-Matic. This offers discrete outputs for each of the six strings.

Imagine you could scream and whisper in all the usual Les Paul voices. Then at a flick of a switch suddenly everything unfolds in 5.1 Dolby Digital surround – the sixth and fifth string boom from a below-stage subwoofer, the first string whispers from stage left and is answered rear right and then pans into centre stage. A Saucer full of Surround Sound Secrets? Axis Digital Bold as Love?

This guitar presents a challenge and it will be interesting to see who has the vision to run with it.

It also has USA-made BurstBuckers with Alnico V magnets – but that's just a beginning!

General description

■ Everything about this guitar declares 'something new'. The bold block blue colour sets the tone.

■ The volume and tone knobs are platinum coloured speed knobs 'back painted'. Note that the bridge pickup volume control doubles as a Digital output master.

■ The three-way switch is platinum plated and unlabelled but serves the usual functions in analogue mode.

■ The humbuckers' pickup covers are platinum plated.

■ The fingerboard is raised unbound ebony with a pronounced attractive grain and 3D block carbon fibre inlays.

■ The guitar is a reasonable 8.75lb (4kg), a surprise in a guitar with extra PU and output options – lighter, in fact, than our Honeyburst Standard at 10.25lb (4.6kg). The body has the vintage sandwich of maple and mahogany. The bottom 'mahogany' layer is one solid piece of timber.

Bridge

Of the newest Tune-O-Matic type, this is a finished in a matching platinum and has the usual thumbscrews for height adjustment. The string length adjustment requires a conventional straight-slot 4.5mm screwdriver accessed, slightly unusually, from the tailpiece side. The unusual retaining spring is only visible from beneath. The stop bar is also platinum plated, bigger than usual, and weighs a substantial 94g.

Neck

This follows a chunky late '50s profile with a fairly constant depth. The neck appears to be one piece, slightly narrower than the 'Standard' at the nut and with a narrow '60s heel and no clumsy volute at the 'weak' headstock junction. The peghead pitch is a nominally standard 17°.

Body

Approximately 50mm thick at the edge binding and 60mm at the highest point of the top carving, similar to the classic vintage Les Pauls which naturally varied. The semi-translucent platinum binding is consistently world class.

■ The unbound ebony fingerboard has 3D carbon fibre block inlays. The fingerboard radius is a traditional 12in. This radius is perfectly matched at the bridge.

■ The truss rod is accessed at the headstock, requiring a '1' point Phillips to remove the platinum truss rod shield, which has the 'HD.6X PRO' logo. The truss rod requires an 8mm socket wrench for any adjustment. The frets are very narrow 2.32mm gauge, marginally narrower than those found on early Les Pauls.

■ The nut seems to be graphite and is perfectly set up for the fitted 'heavy' .011–.050 strings.

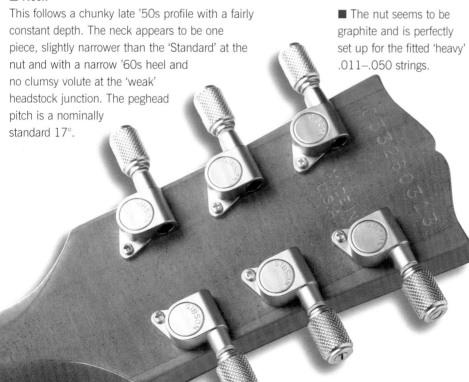

■ The machine heads are unusual 21st-century thumb wheel Gibson types finished in platinum.

■ The headstock has the classic small late '50s profile with a 'separated dot' Gibson logo and glued on 'wings'.

Specific routine maintenance

This guitar arrived beautifully set up and required no adjustment. I suspect that as with other Digital or MIDI guitars the set-up is very critical to the functionality of the HEX pickup and so extra care has been taken at the factory. An instrument of this type will need critical attention if the Digital functions are to remain fully functional. This may mean professional expert attention from time to time.

A factor always worth considering is the string angle between the Tune-O-Matic bridge and the stop tailpiece. Ideally this should be a steep slope to give a good string purchase at the bridge. However, at too steep an angle the strings can snag on the back of the Tune-O-Matic, which may cause premature string breakage as well as unpredictable string slippage. This specific guitar has been well set up with a reasonable .006mm clearance on all strings.

The strings are custom .011–.050, an unusual choice for most modern playing styles, but again probably critical to the function of the HEX pickup, the extra rigidity perhaps giving a more stable and readable tracking for the sophisticated pickup. When changing strings, it's worth checking the machine-head fixing screws, which tend to work loose. This requires a '1' point Phillips. Do not over-tighten them – just enough to stop the machine head moving in normal use.

The locking nuts at the front of the tuners require a 10mm socket spanner and need to be solidly secured.

The machine-head 'tension adjust' screws are an unusual 4.7mm straight-slot screw. These should be slackened for string replacement and re-tightened for tuning stability during normal use.

Whilst you have the tools out it's worth tightening the output panel. This is complicated on this guitar by the inclusion of not one but three outputs – Ethernet, analogue and headphones – and one *input* for a microphone which reappears at the breakout box as an output.

The Ethernet requires a '1' point Phillips, the Classic Mode jack requires the usual 12mm/0.5in socket wrench and the headphones and mike input a 6.8mm knurled ring. The whole panel is secured by four substantial wood screws, and the inputs/outputs are mounted directly to a PCB. Again any problems here are beyond DIY attention and interference would probably void any Gibson warranty.

The guitar is supplied without a scratchplate.

On any instrument the strap buttons are worth checking for secure fitting. If a '2' point Phillips screwdriver can't secure the screw then consider an improvised rawlplug made from a spent matchstick and a little superglue. There were no problems on this new guitar.

The frets are currently beautifully dressed and polished.

Under the hood

Removing the plastic 'platinum-look' rear access panel using the usual '1' point Phillips screwdriver reveals a very clean rout and an impasse! The copper screened and sealed workings of the HD 6X Pro are clearly intended for factory expert attention only and invite no further exploration. The only clues to the complexity of the electronics are the two multiway ribbon cables.

■ The analogue Gibson BurstBucker-type pickups in their custom cases require a 4mm straight-slot screwdriver for adjusting their height in relation to the strings.

■ If for any reason you're removing *all* the strings then an elastic band prevents the loose stop bar falling off and doing damage. A similar tactic is required for the platinum Tune-O-Matic.

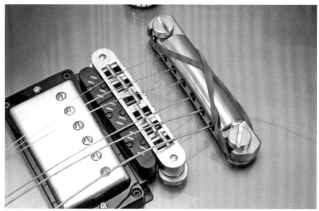

■ When loose, the volume and tone pots require a wrapped-round duster to safely remove the push-fit knob and then a 0.5in socket spanner for removal or adjustment of the pot itself, though any subsequent maintenance is going to be hampered by the sealed unit enclosing the pot itself.

■ Removing the Tune-O-Matic reveals the three-piece modular nature of the HEX pickup. The paired string poles can be adjusted for height and therefore sensitivity using a '0' point Phillips screwdriver.

■ The platinum-coated three-way switch really needs the usual specialist tool for tightening and replacement – the plastic type protects the metal plating from damage.

■ If required, replacing the three-way switch is done via another rear panel (*see 'Replacing a three-way selector', page 44*). A modern 'rounded end' paperclip is a useful gizmo for removing these rear panels as they are often a tight fit even when unscrewed. The rounded end avoids any potential scratching. All the panels are brushed platinum effect on plastic.

■ Revealed by removing the four Phillips '1' point screws the HD 6X also has unusual Gibson USA humbucking pickups. These are undesignated and appear to have balanced wiring as well as a separate screened wire for the Ethernet 'ON' indicator light. Access to the fragile coils is sensibly denied by a soldered seal.

Removing the metal 'cans' or cases is NOT recommended. Though this might look cool it exposes the pickups to environmental damage, will permit some induced hum and will only make the pickups more treble-biased (due to stray capacitance) – the sound of

a Les Paul is warmer tone best left alone. If you want the 'cool' bare pickup look this is easily achieved by buying a set of open case pickups from Seymour Duncan or similar.

The overall pickup height adjustment is effected by two 4mm straight-slot screws attached to a rear metal bracket. 'Springing' is achieved by two substantial springs. The individual pickup pole adjustment requires a 4.5mm straight-slot screwdriver. Take care when reseating humbuckers to ensure their correct orientation – in the case of the neck pickup this means putting the adjustable pole pieces nearest to the fingerboard.

■ The neck pickup cavity reveals the *absence* of the Les Paul signature 'long tenon', making the body probably a current USA 'Standard'. On the original guitars this tenon contributed to the strength of the neck join and the rigidity of the guitar – a key factor in the Les Paul sound. There is, however, substantial weight-relieving routing forming the wiring cavities.

■ Removing the bridge pickup (which is also undesignated) releases and reveals a complex ribbon cable arrangement connecting the HEX pickup.

Specific notes applicable to the HD 6X Pro

It's worth knowing that this guitar can simply be plugged into your favourite amp and wound up to 11 – the original 'plug and play'. However, I experimented with this guitar for a broadcast recording specifically exploring the potential of the six discreet analogue outputs.

Rigging the guitar to the 'Magic' breakout box can merely be a matter of plugging the Ethernet output from the guitar to the Ethernet breakout box input. I'm assured the Ethernet cable *could* be as long as 100m without causing loss of signal or undue 'latency' (digital delay).

The breakout box requires 48V DC at 0.4Amps and this is supplied by the type RA4841N01 mains transformer. The guitar lights up blue at the neck pickup when Ethernet connection is successful and this is mirrored by a green light at the breakout box end.

There are also *input* possibilities at the breakout box consisting of two jacks marked 'to guitar'. These can be used to feed audio to the guitar's headphone output enabling 'in ear' monitoring without extra cabling or wireless connection. These inputs take line level and produce a workable stereo gain at the 3.5mm stereo output on the guitar. This output has it's own dedicated thumb-wheel volume control.

In use

With the six discreet analogue outputs connected to six inputs of an audio mixer the guitar can easily be panned across a conventional stereo image. This produces interesting antiphonal effects, especially when playing repeated arpeggio patterns across the strings. I'm sure there are many more sophisticated possibilities, especially if a 5.1 Dolby rig is available.

Worth noting is the careful audio-level set-up required on the discreet outputs – these are *not* equal as supplied and a 5 to 10dB difference is detected in audio outputs across the individual strings. This setting up needs a little care though. I suspect Magic could line up the outputs to a nominal flat 'equal gain'.

The discreet outputs have a very dry and pure quality which is ideal for sophisticated Digital processing. If used as an analogue source then it responds well to the usual 'audio sweetening' including EQ, reverb, delay and compression.

Another possibility would be a direct Ethernet connection to a computer with recording and MIDI interfaces. The possibilities are endless and I can't help thinking Lester Polfus would have made a lot of this guitar if he'd had it in 1952! He would perhaps have used the microphone and line feeds as he does on his own heavily customised 'Personal' Les Paul. When I asked him he remarked, laughing, that 'Somebody would find a use for it!'

The 3.5mm microphone input on the guitar even has 5V phantom power available for driving capacitor mikes. Perhaps this microphone could pick up your 'voice tube' output for instant Peter Frampton and Jeff Beck FX?

Signed off

The HD 6X required no setting up. Just take care with that Ethernet cable and always replace it with the highest quality 1:1 replacement.

This is a classic Les Paul but with a myriad of other inventive possibilities. I tried it for a radio broadcast exploiting the stereo panning potential, which was well received. I hope that soon somebody will plug one into a stadium-size Dolby 6.1 rig and make the earth move!

Audio can then be *output* at the breakout box, with several options available:

■ 'Classic Mode' analogue from the two humbuckers – 'raw Les Paul' – UNBALANCED or BALANCED (stereo 1/4in)
■ Stereo left and right with strings 123 on the left and 456 on the right (these can of course be reversed) – BALANCED
■ Six discreet outputs one for each individual string – BALANCED – the supplied balanced three-pole cables will interface with a conventional two-pole unbalanced input without undue problems
■ A microphone output – assuming a microphone has been input at the guitar end

Goldtop 'Regular' made in 1953

Serial No. 3 1944

Made in Kalamazoo, Michigan, within the first year of manufacture, this guitar represents a great example of the first viable working Les Paul guitar. Prior to '53 this first Gibson solid guitar had suffered the results of a few misunderstandings between Gibson's design team and musician Les Paul – specifically the bridge/tailpiece neck angle relationship. This makes '52 Goldtops interesting curios but not really gig-friendly guitars.

By 1953 the original trapeze bridge with its curious and impractical 'wrap-under' strings had gone and the neck angle was adjusted to accommodate the new 'wrap-*over*' stud bridge.

This type of Les Paul is seen on the cover of Freddie King's *Hide Away* album and as such marks an important moment in the story of rock and of the now legendary Les Paul guitar. That image and the sound it represented would send Eric Clapton in search of a then discontinued 'obsolete' guitar – the rest, as they say…

General description

■ The volume and tone knobs are manufactured from Tenite Butyrate plastic made by Hughes Tools and Mfg Co, Michigan.

■ The three-way switch has acquired a useful cream plastic surround added in '53 but not found in '52, with the graphics 'rhythm & treble'.

■ The pickups are soapbar P90s in their distinctive cream covers. The eccentrically offset screws found on the '52 have been sorted.

■ The fingerboard is raised bound rosewood with attractive grain.

■ The guitar is a reasonable 8.5lb (3.8kg) – enough weight, however, for the kind of rigidity that produces the distinctive character of the Les Paul sound, Lester's 'railway track with strings'. The body has the vintage sandwich of maple and mahogany. The bottom 'mahogany' layer is one solid piece of timber, missing a little nitro cellulose due to the belt buckles of rock.

■ Bridge

The bridge of the wrap-over '53–'55 type is workable but clearly not easily adjusted for intonation – the Tune-O-Matic was yet to be invented. There are two tiny grub screws which with a 1/16in Allen key enable an approximate adjustment of the string length. Ironically this type of bridge would eventually evolve into the stop bar. The studs are not original and appear to be Badass* replacements. See page 22 for more on the wrap-over bridge.

■ Body

Approximately 50mm thick at the edge binding and only 52.5mm at the highest point of the top carving – much less pronounced than what we think of now as the classic vintage profile, though this naturally varied as a result of hand-sanding. I suspect Gibson were listening to Les Paul, who always preferred a flatter less pronounced carved top. Some late '50s vintage Les Pauls are up to 10mm thicker at the highest point of the top contour! The binding is consistently world class, obviously hand-finished and wearing reasonably well (*see page 23*).

■ Neck

Follows a typically chunky early '50s profile with a fairly constant depth. It is a wonderful piece of mahogany, and is incredibly stable despite the truss rod being so loose that it rattles – not a practical problem, and inaudible electrically. The neck is well played in and has a very narrow profile at the headstock junction. The peghead pitch is a useful 17°. However, Les Paul himself feels this pitch angle is not overly critical. The 'neck set' angle from the body is quite shallow, approximately 3° – more than the 1° angle found on a '52 model but less than the more common 4° found on later Les Pauls.

■ The fully bound fingerboard is of dark close-grained rosewood with mother of pearl trapezoid block inlays. The fingerboard

radius is established at what we now think of as the traditional 12in and perfectly matched at the non-adjustable bridge.

■ The truss rod is accessed at the headstock, requiring a '1' point Phillips to remove the truss rod shield, which is clearly hand-made and, as you'd expect, does *not* have a 'Standard' logo. The shield is an unusual position 10mm from the nut (*see page 25*). This accommodates an early truss rod placement soon altered, which resulted in the familiar 'hard up to the nut' arrangement.

The truss rod requires a standard Gibson 8mm socket wrench for any adjustment. The frets were originally very thin, almost mandolin-like gauge but were badly worn in 1986, at which point the present owner entrusted Bristol-based luthier Jonny Kinkead to re-fret with 0.124in gauge 'chunky' frets. These work well. Jonny also smoothed the worn fingerboard whilst preserving its original radius.

■ The nut is a brass replacement which also works well. The '70s improvement craze is much in evidence!

■ The machine heads are vintage-type 'single ring' Kluson look-alikes with green-tinged 'tulip' pegs. The originals had worn out sometime before 1986 and Dave Gregory fitted these in place of the poor single-type replacements with metal pegs that were in place as he took custody.

■ The headstock has the distinctive small '50s profile with a 'separate dot' Gibson logo.

See pages 20–25 for more on this superb instrument.

Condition on arrival

Much of this guitar has survived 50-odd years of rock'n'roll. It's a little battered cosmetically but the sound is superb. Previously I didn't believe in the mystique surrounding Goldtops, thinking them a poor relation to the humbucking 'bursts. Then I met this one whilst directing the DVD for The Ultimate Guitar Bible. It was played then by its owner, XTC's Dave Gregory. I would strongly recommend checking out this classic sound.

The guitar does have one or two replacement parts but this is what I expect in a practical working instrument of this age. This is not a museum piece.

*The Badass bridge of the 1970s was an important landmark in replacement guitar parts offering viable improvements on traditional designs.

Specific routine maintenance

First check the neck relief with your feeler gauges. The neck should be fairly flat – perhaps .015 relief at the 7th fret given .012in at the 1st fret first string. If the neck does need adjustment, the Goldtop requires an 8mm socket wrench or Gibson guitar tool.

Follow the Vintage Les Paul set-up guide on page 35 for any bridge height and intonation adjustments – the same principles apply, but in a more limited way on this pre-Tune-O-Matic guitar.

The strings on this guitar are D'Addario .011–.048, quite heavy strings. It's a tribute to the set-up that the guitar feels very fluid and supple and has the extra brightness and better intonation associated with heavier strings. When changing strings, it's worth checking the machine-head fixing screws, which tend to work loose. This requires a '1' point Phillips. Do not over-tighten them – just enough to stop the machine head moving in normal use.

Whilst you have the tools out it's worth tightening the output jack retainer. This tends to work loose, causing crackles and intermittent output. Tightening entails removing the square plastic jack socket panel using a '1' point Phillips and getting a grip on the jack socket itself as you tighten the exterior nut with a 12mm/0.5in socket spanner. It may seem a small point but the quality of the screws used on these old guitars is much higher and this makes maintenance so much easier. Dave Gregory prefers to use small jeweller's screwdrivers for adjusting these vintage screws, the idea being that the lower torque afforded by these precision tools means less damage to the ageing metal. Some of the 54-year-old screws *are* becoming a little eccentric.

The guitar is supplied with a rocket tailfin scratchplate of an unusual shape and employs .28mm flat-head screws.

The unusual period strap buttons are worth checking for secure fitting.

Under the hood

Removing the rear access panel using the usual '1' point Phillips screwdriver reveals a very clean rout, and the pots attached directly to the rather nice flame maple. Note the authentic antique components on this mid-20th century guitar – any 1930s radio repairman would be very at home with these parts. The capacitors are very early *pre*-Bumblebee types marked 'TIGER'. Grey Tiger capacitors are found on Gibson guitars made until 1954 and on some '56 models. These are hand-made using foil/film audio capacitors and wax coated.

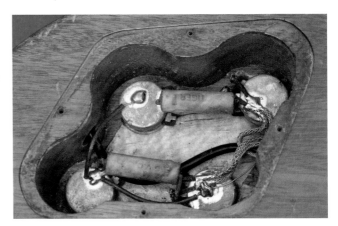

■ The antique wiring is very clean with the four small 500K pots and Tiger 0.022uf capacitors routed to a three-way switch. The pots are all individually coded on their sides:

Bridge tone 134317	Neck tone 134317
Bridge volume 134322	Neck volume 134322

These pots can reliably be dated to early 1953 (17th and 22nd weeks) and the manufacturer is CentraLab (code 134).

■ All the wire is cloth-covered. Most of the wiring is screened using braided earthed looms. The brown backing plates for the control cavities *are* authentic vintage.

■ If loose, the volume and tone pots require a wrapped-round duster to safely remove the push-fit knob and then a 0.5in socket spanner for removal or adjustment of the pot itself. Take care not to catch your fingers on the authentic sharp-edged pointers.

■ The three-way switch really cannot be removed with the normal specialist tool as its small size predates Gibson's standardisation. For tightening and replacement you'll have to resort to a suitably 'softened' set of pliers to protect the metal plating from damage.

■ Replacing the three-way switch is done via another rear panel (*see 'Replacing a three-way selector', page 44*). A modern 'rounded end' paperclip is a useful gizmo for removing these rear panels as they are often a tight fit even when unscrewed. On this old beauty, however, all the panels are 'custom loose'. All the panels are this authentic *brown* plastic with a gloss finish.

■ The Gibson P90-type pickups in their custom cases are not adjustable for height in relation to the strings. The individual pickup pole adjustment requires a .2in straight-slot screwdriver.

■ If for any reason you're removing *all* the strings then an elastic band prevents the loose wrap-over falling off and doing damage.

■ Revealed by removing the two unusual Phillips '1' point screws the Goldtop has classic early P90s. These are undesignated and have interesting zinc backing plates. The pickups have not been wax dipped.

■ The neck pickup cavity reveals the Les Paul signature 'long tenon'. On the original guitars this contributes to the strength of the neck join and the rigidity of the guitar – a key factor in the original Les Paul sound.

Signed off

The Goldtop required no setting up and plays better than any electric guitar I have ever tried. Not all vintage guitars deserve their mystique, but this one does. When wound up through a decent valve combo the guitar delivers something unmistakable! – full of rock'n'roll grit if you want it and the design-concept clean Les Paul 'swing', all through a simple adjustment of gain.

The '53 next to the Epiphone '56.

USA-made 'Deluxe'

Serial No. 73407582*

*In this Gibson eight-number dating system the first and fifth figures represent the year of manufacture.

Made in 1977, this represents a typical example of the 'Deluxe', a guitar originally produced between September 1969 and 1984. It marks an unusual phase in the Les Paul story as it has neither P90 pickups or PAFs but small Epiphone-made mini-humbuckers. These were Epiphone spare stock and conveniently fitted in the existing P90 rout, thus avoiding any factory re-tooling. It seems to have been a response to demand for a Humbucker Les Paul Goldtop. Lester Paul himself told me he liked this model: 'It's still one of my favourites – it sustained so good.'

General description

■ The volume and tone knobs are the gold witches' hat type.

■ The three-way switch has the graphics 'rhythm & treble', which have all but worn off, and an aged golden yellow colour to the plastic knob.

■ The pickup covers are chromium plated, as are almost all the metal parts.

■ The fingerboard is a raised bound rosewood type.

Condition on arrival

Currently the main guitar of Phil Beech of Punk rockers So 77, this guitar has lived the rock'n'roll life and shows the ravages of the road. The original case has taken much of the battering and has actually broken in half. The Goldtop has an unusual 'gig sweat' induced verdigris staining above the bridge pickup, a result of oxidisation of the bronze-based paint, and a hole near the neck joint, probably the aftermath of a re-sighting of the strap button. The mahogany back has also taken a battering from belt-buckles and zips. The rear of the fairly slim neck shows a lot of use, especially in the 1st to 7th positions – the lacquer has discoloured and taken on a matt finish. The guitar will soon require a re-fret.

■ The body is very heavy mahogany with the usual maple cap.

■ Bridge

The bridge of the original ABR-1 Tune-O-Matic type has the usual thumbscrews for height adjustment. The string length adjustment requires a conventional straight-slot 4.5mm screwdriver. The bridge has '50s-type metal saddles but no 'modern' retaining spring.

■ Body

The guitar is a very heavy 5kg, almost 11lb, considerably heavier than a more common maple top reissue. The body thickness is approximately 50mm at the edge binding and 60mm at the highest point of the top carving.

■ Neck

This follows a typical 'slimmer' 1960 profile with a fairly constant depth. It is a three-piece longitudinal sandwich of what appears to be maple!

■ The fully bound fingerboard is high-quality rosewood with real mother of pearl trapezoid block inlays. Its radius is a relatively flat 12in. As found the fingerboard was very dry and responded to a little lemon oil.

■ The truss rod is accessed at the headstock, requiring a '0' point Phillips to remove the truss rod shield with its distinctive 'Deluxe' logo and an 8mm/0.3in wrench for any adjustment. The frets are 2.78mm/.109in gauge and show some uneven wear.

■ The nut is a piece of bone-like plastic which needs some adjustment or replacement, as the owner has changed string gauges to a lighter gauge – consequently the basses are buzzing in their overlarge slots.

■ The machine heads are Kluson-type with elegant 'tulip' tuning pegs.

■ The headstock has the Les Paul signature and a 'separated DOT' Gibson logo, consistent with the period. The headstock angle is 17°.

Specific routine maintenance

First check the neck relief with your feeler gauges. The neck should be fairly flat – perhaps .015 relief at the 7th fret given .012in at the 1st fret first string. If the neck does need adjustment, the '77 requires a specialist 8mm wrench.

Follow the Vintage Les Paul set-up guide (see *page 35*) for any bridge height and intonation adjustments.

It's worth considering the string angle between the Tune-O-Matic bridge and the stop tailpiece. Ideally this should be a steep slope to give a good string purchase at the bridge. However, at too steep an angle the strings can snag on the back of the Tune-O-Matic, which may cause premature string breakage as well as unpredictable string slippage. This specific guitar has exactly that problem. Simply raising the stop bar slightly with a 12mm straight-slot screwdriver will resolve the issue. Interestingly this may also improve the sound and 'feel' of the guitar. Note the flaking chrome and odd screws on the ageing bridge.

The strings on this guitar are .010–.046 Ernie Balls. When changing strings, it's worth checking the machine-head fixing

screws, which tend to work loose. On the '77 this requires a '1' point Phillips. Do not over-tighten them – just enough to stop the machine head moving in normal use.

Whilst you have the tools out it's worth tightening the output jack retainer. This tends to work loose, causing crackles and intermittent output. Tightening entails removing the square metal jack socket using a '1' point Phillips and getting a grip on

the jack screening canister itself as you tighten the bolt with a 13mm/0.5in socket spanner. On this particular guitar the task is made slightly more difficult by the elaborate screening canister that encloses the jack socket. As we will see, the earth screening arrangements on this guitar are very comprehensive.

The scratchplate retaining bracket is best tightened OFF the guitar, as the rear nut is otherwise difficult to adjust without damage to the guitar top. Removing the scratchplate itself requires a '1' point Phillips screwdriver and for tightening the rear nut a 5/16in socket spanner.

The strap lock buttons are worth checking for secure fitting. If a '1' point Phillips screwdriver can't secure the screw then consider an improvised rawlplug made from a spent matchstick and a little superglue.

Under the hood

Removing the rear access panel using the usual '1' point Phillips screwdriver reveals a clean rout. The minimum of wood has been removed. More interesting is the revealed and substantial metal screening cowl that protects the electrical wiring from stray RF and other sources of 'Rattle & Hum'. This is held in place by two machine screws, one of which is missing in action. Removing these gives access to the electrics proper. During these inspections an aerosol lid can make a useful 'screw keep', avoiding accidental losses.

■ The wiring is competent with four classic 500K pots and .02mF capacitors routed to a three-way switch. All the wire is modern PVC-covered. Again the pots are attached to a substantial screening panel and all the wiring is heavily screened using a braided loom.

■ If loose, the volume and tone pots require a wrapped-round duster to safely remove the push-fit knob and then a 0.5in socket spanner for removal or adjustment of the pot itself.

■ The three-way switch really needs a specialist tool for tightening and replacement – the plastic type protects the metal plating from damage. However, the plastic is easily stripped if the nut is too tight! A lot of accumulated grime is revealed under the switch cowl.

■ If required replacing the three-way switch is done via another rear panel (*see 'Replacing a three-way selector', page 44*). A modern 'rounded end' paperclip is a useful gizmo for removing these rear panels as they are often a tight fit even when unscrewed. The rounded end avoids any potential scratching. The existing switch is heavily oxidised but functions just fine, so is best left alone!

■ The small Epiphone humbucker-type pickups in their custom cases require a '1' point Phillips screwdriver for adjusting their height in relation to the strings.

■ If for any reason you are removing *all* the strings then a couple of elastic bands prevent the loose bridge and stop bar falling off and doing damage.

■ Revealed by removing the two Phillips '1' point height adjustment bolts the '77 has authentic USA-made Epiphone mini-humbucking pickups, labelled as 'Williamsville'.* Clearly the pickups have been wax dipped at some point, a measure which often reduces a tendency to high frequency audio feedback. Access to the fragile coils is sensibly denied by a soldered seal. If you feel your pickups may benefit from the wax treatment take them to a specialist – this is not a DIY job as it is so easy to accidentally damage the pickup winding connections and ruin a classic pickup forever.

The overall pickup height adjustment is effected by two bolts attached to a rear metal plate. 'Springing' is achieved by two small pieces of black foam rubber. The individual pickup pole adjustment requires a 3mm straight-slot screwdriver.

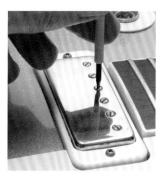

Signed off

The 'Deluxe' requires a little adjustment. The nut problem is attributable to a change of string gauge – the owner previously used hybrid stringing incorporating a heavy set of bass strings. The intonation also requires a tweak. However, this is an impressive guitar which when wound up delivers its own special brand of Kerrang.

The owner likes the guitar 'as it is', dirt and all, so I'm not doing any setting up. Set up or not, it remains a fabulous if rather heavy guitar.

*Possibly a reference to Williamsville, New Jersey.

Epiphone Special
made in China

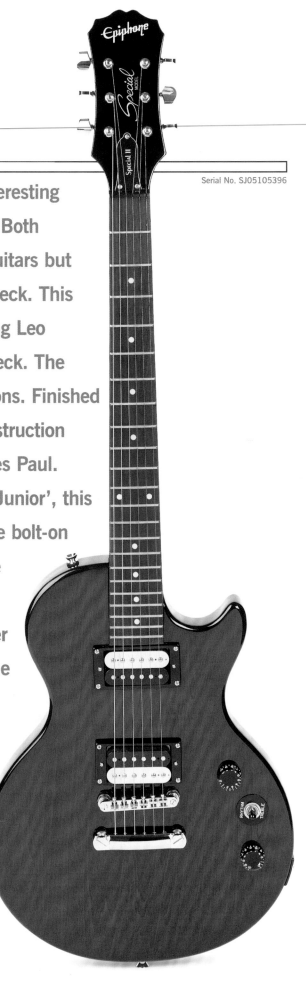

Serial No. SJ05105396

Made in 2006, this guitar represents an interesting departure for the Gibson/Epiphone marque. Both companies have often produced 'student' guitars but always with a traditional luthiers' glued-in neck. This guitar departs from that tradition by adopting Leo Fender's solution of a bolt-on replaceable neck. The guitar has many other 'budget' rationalisations. Finished in a dark cherry, it is of a plywood slab construction missing the maple cap of a thoroughbred Les Paul. Superficially similar to the original student 'Junior', this guitar makes a fine 'first electric guitar'. The bolt-on neck has the popular thin 1960 profile. The guitar is also reminiscent of the Gibson 'Melody Maker', but with humbuckers rather than a P90 pickup. It has two Chinese-made humbuckers.

I decided to leave SGs, Melody Makers and Juniors out of this book as they are different enough to warrant their own manual. However, the unusual neck and other features persuaded me to retain this one nod to the *other* Les Pauls.

General description
■ The guitar has a rationalised set of *one* volume and *one* tone knob of the 'Speedknob' clear top with black base type.
■ The three-way switch is moved from its traditional position to sit between the tone and volume and has the usual graphics 'rhythm & treble'.

■ The pickups are without covers and of a zebra type with mixed bobbins.

■ The fingerboard is a raised *un*bound hardwood.

■ The guitar is a relatively light 8.25lb (3.75kg), ideal for a young student.

■ Bridge

The Epiphone-type zinc alloy Tune-O-Matic designated 'B2', is slightly more substantial, less eccentric and possibly better engineered than the hand-built Gibson originals. It has the usual thumbscrews for height adjustment as well as the modern screw top adjust option.

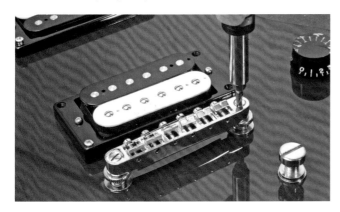

■ The string length adjustment requires a conventional straight-slot 4.5mm screwdriver accessed from the pickup side.

■ The bridge has chrome-plated saddles and has a 'modern' retaining spring. The stop bar is *not* weight-reducing aluminium as found on the original '60 guitar but an inexpensive cast alloy which is nevertheless lightweight at 74g. The stop bar is set into the body with two height adjustable bolts.

■ Body

The unusual plywood body is a thin 40mm at the unbound edges and of a totally flat slab type with NO archtop.

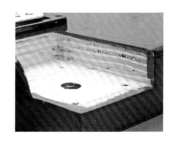

■ Neck

Follows a typical 'slimmer' 1960 profile with a fairly constant 20mm depth. The neck appears to be of two-piece construction with the headstock jointed at the 2nd fret. This is an economy but unlikely to cause undue problems, as a glued joint can be stronger than wood grain. It has virtually no heel due to the bolt-on construction. This also avoids a clumsy volute at the traditionally 'weak' headstock junction. The jointed neck means that a budget use of wood still allows for a peghead pitch at a useful 17°.

■ The unbound fingerboard is of a dark stained wood with simple 'dot' inlays. The unusual 'compound' fingerboard radius is an equally unusual 14in at the nut, getting even flatter at the neck joint.

■ The truss rod is accessed at the headstock, requiring a '1' point Phillips to remove the two-ply truss rod shield, which has a 'Special 2' logo. The truss rod requires a 4mm Allen wrench for any adjustment. The frets are narrow 2.77mm gauge.

■ The nut is a piece of black plastic which needs a little setting up.

■ The machine heads are modern chromium-plated, unbolted, unadjustable economy types.

■ The headstock retains the distinctive Epiphone 'small' profile with a silver decal logo.

Condition on arrival

This new guitar is supplied in a cardboard box with an economy guitar lead and no frills.

Specific routine maintenance

First check the neck relief with your feeler gauges. The neck should be fairly flat – perhaps .015 relief at the 7th fret given .012in at the 1st fret first string.

Follow the Vintage Les Paul set-up guide (*page 35*) for any bridge height and intonation adjustments except for raising the Tune-O-Matic, which has the unusual 'top screw' option making for easier raising if needed. This requires a 4mm straight-slot screwdriver. Epiphone recommends 4/64in clearance at the treble side 12th fret and 6/64in at the bass side.

A factor worth considering is the string angle between the Tune-O-Matic bridge and the stop tailpiece. Ideally this should be a steep slope to give a good string purchase at the bridge. However, at too steep an angle the strings can snag on the back of the Tune-O-Matic, which may cause premature string breakage as well as unpredictable string slippage. This specific guitar has been well set up with a good .042mm clearance on the sixth string.

The unusual bolt-on neck should be a tight fit and requires a '2' point Phillips for any tightening. The snug accurate fit on this particular guitar requires no corrective shims as the neck is set at a good workable angle to the body.

The strings on this guitar are .010–.046, a common choice for this shorter scale guitar. When changing strings, it's worth checking the machine-head fixing screws, which tend to work loose. This requires a '1' point Phillips. Do not over-tighten them – just enough to stop the machine head moving in normal use.

Whilst you have the tools out it's worth tightening the output jack retainer. This tends to work loose, causing crackles and intermittent output. Tightening entails removing the square plastic jack socket panel using a '1' point Phillips and getting a grip on the jack socket itself as you tighten the exterior nut with a 12mm socket spanner.

The guitar is supplied without a scratchplate. The strap buttons are worth checking for secure fitting. If a '1' point Phillips screwdriver can't secure the screw then consider an improvised rawlplug made from a spent matchstick and a little superglue.

If, as in this case, the frets need a little polish then a simple cardboard template and some light abrasive such as Planet Waves fret polishing paper will do the trick. Similarly, the fingerboard *may* benefit from a little lemon oil.

Under the hood

Removing the single rear access panel using the usual '1' point Phillips screwdriver turns out to be a bit of a nightmare. The panel is a little small and remains stuck in the recess. The safe way to remove a stuck panel

without damaging the plate or the guitar is to use a large screw as a makeshift handle – screwed in lightly it should grip the plastic without cracking, but be careful! The rout revealed is very tight with just enough space for the two pots and switch. The rear of the plastic panel is screened with foil and the cavity with conductive black paint. During these inspections a recycled container can make a useful 'screw keep', avoiding accidental losses.

■ The wiring is reasonably clean with two small modern 500K pots and one .02mF capacitor routed to a three-way switch. All the wire is modern PVC-covered.

■ If loose, the volume and tone pots require a wrapped-round duster to safely remove the push-fit knob and then a 12mm socket spanner for removal or adjustment of the pot itself.

■ The three-way switch really needs a specialist tool for tightening and replacement – the plastic metric-size type protects the metal plating from damage.

■ If required, replacing the three-way switch is done via the same rear panel (*see 'Replacing a three-way selector', page 44*). The panel is authentic black plastic with a gloss finish.

■ The humbucker-type pickups in their open cases require a '1' point Phillips screwdriver for adjusting their height in relation to the strings.

■ If for any reason you are removing *all* the strings then an elastic band prevents the loose stop bar falling off and doing damage.

■ Revealed by removing the four Phillips '1' point screws, the Special 2 has two humbucking pickups. These are designated 'Neck pickup' and 'BHC' (the bridge pickup), presumably a type of BurstBucker. If the pickups *have* been wax dipped there is no sloppy excess revealed around the case. Access to the fragile coils is sensibly denied by a soldered seal.

The overall pickup height adjustment is effected by two '1' point Phillips screws attached to a rear metal bracket. 'Springing' is achieved by two substantial springs. The individual pickup pole adjustment requires a 4mm straight-slot screwdriver – these are best adjusted, however, with the strings in place. Generally a specific pole may be adjusted *down* to reduce the output of a string that stands out from the mix. Take care when reseating humbuckers to ensure their correct orientation – in the case of the neck pickup this means putting the cream zebra nearest to the fingerboard.

Signed off

The Special 2 required a little setting up. The nut could be filed a little lower and the Tune-O-Matic could also come down a little, but this is all to be expected in a budget guitar. The stop bar lugs were also a little loose, which may result in a loss of tone, easily remedied with a large screwdriver suitably scratchproofed with electrical tape. A little lemon oil on the very dry fingerboard may help. However, this budget guitar delivers something very like the Junior sound – perhaps a little *hotter* due to the modern overwound BurstBuckers.

Custom Shop Peter Frampton 'Signature Model'

Essentially a three-pickup 'Custom', Peter Frampton's signature guitar has some interesting distinguishing features which merit attention – especially it's almost semi-acoustic body.

General description

■ The three-PU 'Custom' is an interesting guitar which has appeared in the hands of guitarists Jimmy Page and Keith Richards amongst others. Peter Frampton sometimes used a regular 'Custom' during his late '60s/ early '70s heyday. Coupled with a 'voice tube' it became one of the most distinctive sounds of the 1970s, and *Frampton Comes Alive* is still the biggest selling live album of all time. Peter clearly loved the sound of two adjacent pickups used simultaneously – 'the snarl' as Leo Fender called it – and with the standard 'Custom' this was only possible on the bridge and middle combination, the middle position of the pickup selector.

However, though finished and fully bound just like a regular 'Custom' the body of this guitar is a 'Standard' configuration with a maple cap on an unusual semi-hollow mahogany back. It is 'weight-relieved' to 8.5lb (3.8kg) compared with 9lb (4kg) for a typical two-pickup 'Custom'. A cat scan of the guitar reveals its ES335-like structure.

For his signature 'Custom' Peter has elected to have the middle pickup permanently switched ON. This makes available the bridge and middle pickups (position 1 Lead), all three pickups (position 2 Centre) and middle and neck pickups (position 3 Rhythm). Additionally the 'bottom' volume control operates the gain on the middle pickup, meaning that you can effectively turn this PU off, making available the neck on its own, the bridge on its own and the bridge and neck together – nifty! The other volume control gives you the option to blend the outer two pickups with the middle.

An X-ray reveals the semi-acoustic nature of the Frampton guitar.

142

■ His three pickups are 'un-canned', which means without the metal covers the consequential stray inductance will result in a lift in the high frequency spectrum.

■ The pickups have cream surrounds for the appearance of a cool non-zebra 'DiMarzio' upgrade effect.

■ The guitar has 'Speedknobs', not traditional witches' hats, for tone and volume.

■ The individually specified slim-profile neck has 'Custom-style' block oblong fingerboard inlays and single-ply binding, with Pete Frampton's signature at the 12th fret.

■ The 'Nashville' Tune-O-Matic has modern individual saddle retaining springs.

■ The 'gold'-plated stop bar weighs a fairly substantial 87g and has no retaining springs, so use a rubber band to keep it in place when changing strings.

■ The guitar is strung with .009–.044in – light for a Les Paul but very satisfying, and with no loss of punch.

Under the hood

■ The electrics are all modern well soldered components with PVC wiring.

■ The extent of the 'weight relief' cavity is quite staggering – that's 8in of ruler disappearing into the control cavity! Almost the same applies moving towards the pickups. The bottom of the control cavity is also carved out and a full 14in of ruler disappears into the switch compartment. This is getting on for being a small ES335 semi-acoustic.

■ The cavities are painted black, but disappointingly this is *not* screening paint.

■ The guitar has the fabled 'long tenon' at the neck joint and 'gold pole' PAF humbuckers – two '57 classics and a 500T.

Signing off

Acoustically this guitar sounds very resonant, 'woodier' and less nasal (middle frequency accented) than a traditional solid mahogany 'Custom'. Plugged in this is a very versatile guitar. On the 'clean' channel of a Fender Hot Rod Deluxe it delivers crisp country tones – *not* Telecaster 'bite', more Chet Atkins, and also with the neck pickup and tone controls in circuit 'jazz mellow'. In the drive channel of the amp you get all the usual Les Paul 'grunt' with endless sustain. The myriad pickup combinations are very interesting and the minute phase errors introduced by three pickups in different positions all working together is ideal for getting the most from a chorus effect or any time-related FX.

Condition on arrival

This particular Frampton guitar belongs to Gibson Artist Relations London, and has seen a little life in the hands of celebrity Gibson endorsee guitarists. It is fairly well set up and plays like a working instrument straight out of the box. I would suggest lifting the stop bar a few millimetres as the strings catch the back of the Tune-O-Matic, stifling the strings a little. Also the nut is a little high and the Tune-O-Matic a little low – the intonation needs setting for .009s, the guitar is factory set for .010s. A good working instrument.

USA-made 'Robot'
Tronical self-tuning guitar

Whilst Haynes manuals normally confine advice to production models the 'Robot' offers a fascinating glimpse at a potential future for the electric guitar. In the 18th century Dr Johnson observed that lutenists spent half their life playing their instrument and the other half tuning it. By the 21st century little had changed. However, in 2007 Gibson, with German company Tronical, developed a self-tuning Les Paul. This not only tunes itself to standard tuning at concert pitch but also offers quick retuning to the following alternate settings:

■ Open tuning E major EBEG#BE
■ DADGAD
■ Dropped D – DADGBE
■ Open G – GBDGBD
■ Hendrix/Stevie Ray Vaughan Eb Ab Db Gb Bb Eb
■ Double Dropped D – DADGBD

These are factory preset options based on using .010 gauge strings, but other custom options *are* programmable.

The retuning options are real, not 'virtual', and are achieved by a combination of electrical and mechanical processes. Sophisticated computer electronics 'listen' to each string via an extra Tune-O-Matic-mounted piezo pickup and calculate any

required tuning adjustment. This information is conveyed via a tiny ribbon cable to an 8-bit microprocessor installed in the guitar body. This compares the measured frequency with the desired 'in-tune' frequency and sends the resulting control signal up to a second microprocessor.

The second microprocessor then operates the servo motors controlling the machine heads, with any adjustments required being made and checked by six brushless DC motors.

General description

In many respects this is a regular American 'Standard' Les Paul finished, in this instance, in 21st-century blue. The unbound 'no frills' body, the oversize tuners and 'odd MCK/tone knob' coupled with transparent access panels are the only visible signs of something radical. The Tune-O-Matic and stop tail are also slightly larger and contain a piezo pickup and pre-amp.

The Powertune auto tuning process for standard tuning step by step

Instantly activated tuning mode

■ On pulling the custom tone knob 'out' (it's a push-pull pot with an additional centre push-activated button called by Gibson the MCK or 'master control knob'), all the strings are indicated on the pots' in-built LEDs as red, indicating 'not yet tuned'.

■ Just strumming the strings gently *once* sets the servo motors in the machine heads turning and achieves E, G and E in tune, all in about three seconds. These light up green on the MCK LEDs, indicating 'in tune'.

■ You can then hone in and play the A, D and B strings, which still display red, and these will tune up in about three seconds each. The LEDs will then all flash blue, indicating 'all in tune'. A 'refresh' tune of the guitar when left unplayed for 24 hours typically takes about seven seconds.

■ You should then deactivate the system by pushing the MCK 'in' (if you forget to do this it will switch off automatically after two minutes).

■ If custom-tempered tuning is required de-clutch the servo concerned by pulling the relevant tuning peg away from the headstock and adjust by ear. This custom-tempered tuning can, if required, be saved to one of the presets.

Perhaps the most useful aspect of this guitar is being able to get to non-standard tuning quickly, eg auto tuning from standard to DADGAD:

■ First activate the system by pulling up the tone knob as before and turning the custom knob until the 'A' LED is displayed.

■ Gently push the centre section of the knob and strum the strings as above. DADGAD tuning will be achieved in about 30 seconds.

From a maintenance point of view one feature that sets the guitar apart is the fact that the Tune-O-Matic contains a lot of electronics and is not user-serviceable. Like a lot of electronics these days it is most likely built around a 'replacement only' philosophy.

Auto tuning in practice
Auto tuning works within expected limits:

■ There is a steep learning curve with this guitar, as with any computer-assisted device. To take advantage of the sophisticated facilities there is a lot to learn, and the use of multi-function controls means you'll need to read the specific Gibson manual supplied with the guitar to get the most from this and subsequent upgrades. For example, there are optional levels of tuning accuracy within the range .2 cent to 2.5 cent – this is programmable via the same single custom knob. The trade-off is accuracy against time taken. You can choose to be less discriminating on stage, where tuning time is critical, and also perhaps be more discerning in a recording situation where time is sometimes less pressing.

■ It will tune to a nominal EADGBE fairly quickly in it's simplest mode. This will suffice for strumming a pop song or knocking out a few power chords.

■ This is as ever only a starting point for accurate key-tempered guitar tuning in any critical situation, such as recording.

Manual fine-tuning and custom-tempered tuning is possible, by disengaging individual strings from the Tronical system. This is mechanically achieved by de-clutching the tuning keys from the servo mechanism by physically pulling them away from the headstock as above.

Using Powertune to assist intonation setting
Aside from tuning, the Powertune system also has a mode that helps players intonate the guitar – essentially a string-length optimisation that helps the guitar play in tune up and down the neck. Many guitarists intonate the guitar themselves, making adjustments to the bridge saddle locations until the fretted and harmonic notes at the 12th fret, the midpoint of the vibrating string, match for each string. See page 40 for more on this. With Powertune's intonation mode, the system uses lights on its LED to guide the user through the process of making the necessary manual adjustments by turning the screws on the Tune-O-Matic.

The Powertune system uses rechargeable batteries in the form of two AA NMH cells. With a capacity of 2100mAh, the batteries are good for about 200 tunings. Recharging is achieved 'in guitar' by a clever dual use of the guitar's output jack.

Although the self-tuning system's Powerhead tuners contain a 0.5Nm brushless DC motor, a release mechanism for manual tuning and an 18:1 worm-drive to make the string tension adjustments, they still fit into the same space as a traditional high-end manual tuning head. At just 46.5g the Powerhead tuners are about 2.5gm *lighter* than their manual counterparts.

Retro-fit
It is possible to buy a complete Tronical system for your existing Les Paul. In 2008 this kit comes in at approximately £500. However, please resist the temptation to make such radical alterations to a vintage guitar.

Maintenance
The most likely fault with the tuning system will probably be damage to the Powerhead servo mechanisms. If the guitar is handled by anybody unaware of the servo mechanism it is very likely to be damaged. The guitarist's natural instinct to manually adjust the tuning pegs must be resisted.

The machine head servos *must* be disengaged before manual tuning is attempted – this is a simple operation, but imperative.

Damaged servos will require replacement or expert repair.

Changing strings
The 'Robot' has special modes for changing strings, accessed via the MCK:
■ 'String down', which unwinds *all* the strings.
■ 'String up', which takes all the strings up to near pitch. This mode can be assigned to individual strings for replacement after breakage.

Replacing a single string is achieved as normal except that the individual Powertune must be de-clutched from the servo motor for any adjustment. Also all the individual strings have locking screws which require unlocking for removal of the old string.

The new string is locked in place by tightening the thumb screw. The locking facility allows for the fact that the strings cannot have much of a winding on the pegs. This is because the strings mustn't touch and short-circuit each other. For the same reason the strings must be cut short, allowing no excess

beyond the individual peg head. Presumably they carry some discrete information to the servos. Provided string contact is made with the Tune-O-Matic saddle, automatic 'string up' can be assigned to that string using the usual MCK. Fine tuning is then operated as usual.

In use
My personal take on the 'Robot', or indeed a retrofit Powertune guitar, is that it could be very useful in the sort of stage musical 'pit' orchestra situation I've often encountered. Here lots of segues and a very exposed performance environment leave little opportunity for re-tuning, and yet tuning is often very exposed and critical.

Another situation might be a class teaching environment. Here the teacher is often too busy to tune his own guitar mid class and doing so would leave the class open to distraction. I could imagine setting the guitar off to check its own tuning whilst the teacher focuses a class on the next arrangement – useful, if currently expensive.

I feel this prototype still requires a little minor refinement, particularly in the area of being a little more robust. I'm not totally convinced it is yet rugged enough for a stage rock guitar. However, I'm sure this exciting development will soon prove useful. If the economy of scale could be made to work this would be a fantastic facility on entry-level guitars where beginners really do need help with tuning.

Gibson should be applauded for this daring enterprise which is very much in the innovative Les Paul spirit.

'Greeny' Peter Green's USA-made '59

Serial No. 9 2038

This guitar has in the past belonged to both Peter Green and Gary Moore. Peter used it for most of his Fleetwood Mac recordings and Gary Moore used it for *Blues For Greeny* as well as many other landmark recordings. Peter bought it in Selmers on London's Charing Cross Road in 1966 for £110, *second-hand*. The guitar is in 2008 owned by Phil Winfield, president of Maverick Music USA. This is perhaps the Holy Grail of 'burst '59s. Though famously described by Peter himself as 'no magic stick' it is nevertheless the guitar that helped inspire some of the most heartfelt electric blues of the 20th century.

Condition on arrival

As you can see from the photographs, this is a well-used guitar. It has a repaired fracture of the neck (the result of a car accident whilst owned by Gary Moore), a missing scratchplate (missing since 1968), a broken pickup selector and lots of missing lacquer, as well as an ultraviolet-faded sunburst verging on natural. It came to Phil in Gary Moore's flight case, which contained some other small accessories. Phil now plays it a few times a week.

Perhaps the most intriguing aspect of this guitar is its 'out of phase' pickups.

Jol Dantzig of Hamer guitars told me: 'My observation of the guitar in the '80s took place over two days while Gary was in Chicago visiting my shop. I was designing some guitars for him so naturally the subject of the "Greeny" Les Paul came up.

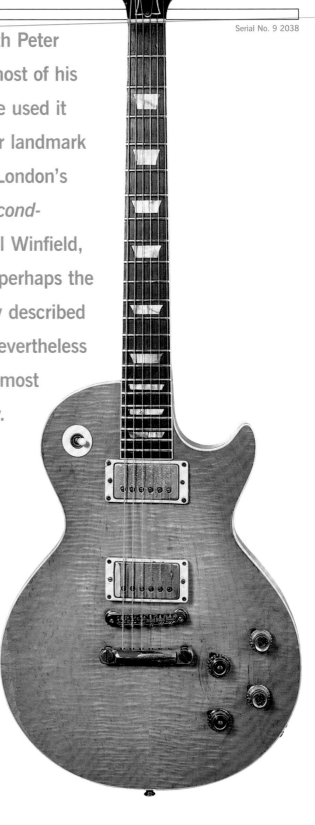

'We talked about the middle position tone, and how it was so different from other Les Pauls. I mentioned to him that since about 1977 I had built the Hamer guitars wired out-of-phase in my desire to approach the "Peter Green" sound. Having owned several original 'bursts myself, I was curious to know if the pickups were intentionally wired differently or if it was just happenstance. Luckily, Gary trusted me, and encouraged me to take the guitar apart so that we might discover the answer.

'My inspection indicated that the neck pickup hadn't been messed with at all except to have been turned around in the cavity. The solder joints holding the cover onto the chassis of the pickup were original and the cover didn't show any signs of the flexing that can occur when someone removes it, then puts it back on. From these observations (and based upon my personal experience of having disassembled scores of original pickups) I concluded that the magnet had merely been inserted the wrong way around when the pickup was manufactured. A quick test with a magnetic compass proved this out. One magnet was orientated north to south while the other was orientated south to north. The pickups were magnetically out of phase.

'In addition, both of the pickups' coax appeared to have original and have unmolested solder joints inside the control cavity as well. The reversed magnetic polarity of the neck pickup created the famous "Peter Green" out-of-phase sound when the guitar was played with both pickups on. I spent quite a bit of time playing the guitar over two days, and "The Sound" was easy to recreate. Being a huge Fleetwood Mac fan, you can understand how thrilling this was for me. Interestingly, I didn't even think of asking him to sell it to me!'

It would seem then that a happy accident caused this fascinating arrangement. The difference between this out-of-phase effect and wiring two pickups out of phase is subtle but important. With magnetic polarity phase-shift the extent of 'cancellation' seems to vary with audio frequency, leaving low frequencies relatively intact whilst high frequencies have a pronounced hollow ring.

The original Klusons with their distinctive 'tulip' pegs have been replaced with modern Sperzels – a probable improvement in tuning stability for what is a working guitar.

The pickup selector switch knob is 'part missing in action', and the owner has wisely decided to leave the original switch in situ.

The Bumblebee capacitors made by Sprague are a distinctive feature of the

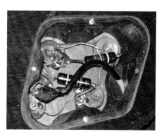

'58–'60 'bursts and are felt by many experts to contribute to the distinctive sound of these vintage guitars. Gibson have taken this on board and use facsimiles in their current VOS guitars. Confusingly Sprague originally called these capacitors 'Black Beauties', a name which has the other connotation of the Custom 'Black Beauty' Les Paul guitar.

The tone and volume pots seem original, though it is difficult to be certain – they are certainly of the right type and value and also do the job! I was not able to do pot number checks.

The neck of this guitar has a distinctive long tenon extending so far into the body that it is visible under the neck pickup cavity. This long tenon is felt to be a major contributor to the rigidity and 'interference neutrality' of the Les Paul design – the guitar should move as little as possible, thereby allowing the pickup to 'hear' the string, and not random cancellations caused by body-induced pickup vibration. This is an interesting area and sparks a debate (*see page 10 for more on this*).

The finish on this original '59 guitar is of course nitro-cellulose and extremely ultraviolet faded, especially in the red spectrum. The red pigments Gibson used at this time were prone to rapid deterioration, and like so much else about the classic 'bursts accidentally results in a tasteful 'lemon drop' finish as apposed to the original garish red sunburst.

Signed off

At the time this, and the other 1,711 classic 'bursts were made, each guitar was handmade by a team of perhaps 12 people. It shows. With a little maintenance this guitar is good for another couple of hundred years and will hopefully find its way into the hands of other great players.

Key Les Paul players and their guitars

Alongside the Fender Stratocaster the Les Paul is one of the great icons of rock. More than its Stratospheric rival the Les Paul epitomises four very specific sounds: the intended clear jazzy pop sound epitomised in Les Paul himself, a deep warm blues that can also 'bite' as in Freddie King or *Beano*-era Clapton, an out-of-phase vocal breathiness as in Peter Green and Gary Moore, and the heart of the overdriven power chord as in Spinal Tapping heavy metal.

In the following chapter I have researched the guitars and gear of some of the most prominent Les Paul players. We need to remember that there are often as many as ten stages in the sound chain from the inspired touch of a great player to the loudspeakers in an auditorium or our MP3 players. These stages involve other individuals such as guitar techs, sound engineers, producers and mastering engineers, as well as all the equipment they employ in their own brand of alchemy.

To what extent is the Les Paul mythology justified? How important is the vintage or ageing factor? What can we learn from the specific guitars, amplification FX and recording procedures of the legendary Les Paul players?

LEFT Les Paul legends.

RIGHT The beauty of the 'burst.

Les Paul

aka Lester William Polfus

Heavily modified Les Paul 'Personal', serial number lost

It's too easy to forget that Les Paul *the guitarist* came first, long before the eponymous guitar, Lester was a star as early as the 1940s, when he became an accompanist to the first 20th-century pop star, Bing Crosby. In 1945 they had a number one hit together with *It's Been a Long Long Time*.

Ironically most of Les Paul's chart successes, including 1951 US number one *How High The Moon*, were recorded on prototype guitars which Lester built himself that he calls 'logs' and 'klunkers'. They were 'bitsa' instruments, using bits of Epiphone and Gibson guitars, often with a fingerboard by Larson.

The central theme of these guitars, however, became the search – started in 1941 – for a guitar with a solid core. For some of these prototypes, the 'logs', this was crudely but effectively achieved utilising 4in by 4in batons, to which Lester added conventional Epiphone guitar sections for purely aesthetic reasons.

Lester describes, in his introduction to this book, how he came to take such drastic steps. He has also consistently advocated low-impedance 'Hi Fidelity' pickups, for their pure 'flat' sound. In 2007 I asked him about his love of low-impedance pickups:

'You're a lot of times working where they have neon signs and a lot of interference, and with my [low-impedance] guitar I don't care what direction I face in, I don't have any problems. And the second thing is that if I'm working for the President and I have to run a cable 50-feet long, *I* don't have a problem with 50 feet but the *other* guitar player, he's sweating [*laughs*] – he's got a terrible time on his hands because he's only allowed at most a couple of feet and he's in trouble. So, high-impedance? – it never should have been there but it's there.

'I got the idea from the telephone company. The telephone company has

A Les Paul 'Personal' – the '69 version – a guitar in a state of constant evolution.

been low-impedance since it started, broadcasting and everything else, and there's very few things that can work high-impedance.'

How does that knock on to the rest of the electronics in the guitar?

'You've got big problem, and that is the whole world makes their amplifiers high-impedance, so I said "Are we going to go out and change the world?" I don't think so! I said "Let someone else change the world".'

So you put a transformer on the guitar to convert it to high-impedance?

'Yeah [*laughs*]! We made the second mistake by placing it in the wire, so if you don't remember to take the special cable you can't play the guitar.'

So, how does that figure with the Les Paul 'Personal'? That's fairly close to the guitar you use yourself, isn't it?

'Yeah, we just lightened it up. It wasn't necessary to go nearly that heavy or anything, those were the first ones and of course when you made those things you needed two trucks to carry them on!'

So the stock 'Personal' that they sell over the counter, is that close to the one you use?

'Yeah, same thing.'

When you were trying to get the original Les Paul together, how important was the headstock angle?

'I don't think it's important, not at all! – as long as there's enough slant on it. Gibson liked the low heel at the joining of the head to the neck, and it made no difference to me at all. So those are things that are trivial. If there is a difference it's minute.'

Lester playing his heavily modified
Les Paul 'Personal'.

The sandwich you get with mahogany and maple on the carved-top guitars, how important is that to the sound?

'Well the mahogany will contribute a warmer sound, meaning mainly that it's being interfered with by the string, the vibration of the string and what it's attached to. Now the more that you enter into colouration – and colouration is a big problem that you're going to have, because if you build two guitars alike they won't sound alike – that's a problem all of it's own to deal with. So you try your darndest to make sure that nothing vibrates that doesn't *have* to vibrate.'

As an inventor and guitarist striving for a very pure 'clean' tone, Les Paul has always advocated rigidity and neutrality in the substance of his instruments – particularly the neck:

'There are certain things like the neck on the guitar that vibrate despite of what happens. There's that string across there and when you pluck that string that's vibrating that neck. Of course, if the neck's made of the finest material you can get that *doesn't* vibrate, then you're better off.'

So you don't get too much cancellation?

'Yeah, but then there are those that say "Oh I love that *woody* sound," and there's nothing wrong with them, if they're lucky enough to find something that gives them their wishes. It's how much sugar they want to add to their coffee.

'The first thing we considered was sustain. The purpose of the model was to sustain without having to smother a note or pick the string twice. And it needed to be even, long, and with distinctive decay. It had the right combination of mahogany and maple, and pickups.'

Lester has similar views on amplifiers, favouring the engineers' amplifier ideal of 'a length of wire with gain'. These principles work well for him, but ironically fly in the face of all that has made the '58–'60 'bursts famous.

The most famous Les Paul sounds – those of Clapton's *Beano* album, Peter Green's *Need Your Love So Bad*, Mike Bloomfield's *Super Session*, Paul Kossof's *All Right Now* – all

these rely on 'colouration', whether induced by out-of-phase pickups, overdriven Marshall amplifiers, Dallas Rangemaster treble boosters, accidentally over-wound and frequency-skewed PAFs, overdriven valve-powered EMT echo plates or the resonance of a particular piece of maple mahogany sandwich.

It seems the human ear savours the idiosyncrasies and 'distortions' that computers and science find *so far* almost impossible to predict and emulate. If this were *not* true, the world's music factories would be churning out Stradivarius violins and '58–'60 'bursts at discount prices – which, of course, they are not.

Inevitably we are also exploring the all-important human factor. As has already been mentioned, most '58–'60 'bursts were made by as few as 12 luthier craftsmen, and the guitars they produced are all subtly different.

The biggest factor however, is best described in Les Paul's own words: 'The final element of my secret is the part I can't do anything about because it comes down to the way *you* play, and what *you* are feeling when you play it. I can pick up anybody's guitar, and there it is. It's in *your* fingers, it's in *your* head it's in what *you* get out of what you've got.

'So a guy says, "I'm playing the same guitar you play, I'm playing the same things you play and I've got the amplifier set just right. So how come I don't get that big ballsy sound?"

'And I can only tell him, "Well you're not me…Figure it out!"'

Freddie King

'53 Goldtop, serial number unknown

In 1966 Freddie King inspired Eric Clapton to buy a new guitar and unknowingly started the whole Les Paul revival. Ironically Clapton bought a 1960 'Standard' – the nearest thing he could find to the guitar Freddie is pictured with on the cover of his album *Let's Hide Away and Dance Away*. Clapton was likely learning *Hide Away*, which he famously featured in his 'Clapton is God' period and, of course, recorded himself on the groundbreaking *Beano* album.* He clearly realised that his Telecaster into a Vox AC30 combination was not really cutting it for Texas blues, and anyway, the Telecaster belonged to The Yardbirds, whom he had just left!

Freddie King had been born in 1934 in Longview, Texas, a world away from Surrey, and moved to Chicago in the significant year of 1950, young, hungry and in the right place at exactly the right time. Turned down by Chess for sounding too much like the other King, 'Blues Boy' Riley King, it was ten long, mean, blues years until he made an album – ten years of soaking up the juice with fellow Chicago drifters Magic Sam, Muddy Waters, Hubert Sumlin and Howlin' Wolf, the University of The Blues incarnate.

When he cooked up *Hide Away* with pianist Sonny Thompson for Federal record '12401' in August 1960, Freddie was a true pioneer. In a Cincinnati studio and playing a seven-year-old 1953 Goldtop into a small Fender valve combo at restrained sound levels, Freddie produced a classic single coil P90 'sting' with the merest suggestion of valve compression and soft, even harmonic, peak distortion. The stop tail wrap-over bridge meant that Freddie could palm mute the strings for the boogie sections in a way that was impossible on the '52 Les Paul with its bizarre 'wrap-under' arrangement.

According to Lightning Red, Freddie used 'a heavier gauge set of strings plucked by this big man's thumb – Freddie preferred not to use a pick, and I believe this contributed to his string-bending vibrato being much slower than BB King's.' However, Freddie himself said 'I don't use a straight pick. I use a steel pick on my index finger and a plastic pick on my thumb…I saw Muddy Waters doing this.'

In his later career Freddie is seen with a range of guitars including a sunburst Les Paul 'Deluxe' with mini-humbuckers. For amps he favoured Fender twins and Super reverbs and later on he used Fender Quad Reverb – all wound up to 10! John Mayall recalls him getting his sound out of anything and never using an FX pedal. When Freddie toured the UK in the 1960s Fender amps were, of course, extremely rare.

Freddie died tragically young on 28 December 1976, but he left a legacy in sound that changed electric guitar playing forever.

*Ironically when I first heard this album in the Liverpool of 1966, all the Mersey musicians revered Clapton's outrageous guitar tone, but the repertoire itself seemed a real step back – many had been covering Ray Charles songs for ten years. But 1966 was the year of *Revolver* and the beginnings of psychedelia. Jeff Beck, now in Eric Clapton's Yardbirds shoes, was pushing the guitar's soundworld into daring feedback experiments and structurally inventing 'progressive rock'. The 'Beano' album then seemed a really strange album. But of course, it went to number six in the charts, stuck around for 16 weeks and launched a healthy late '60s blues revival, inspiring a search for the roots of rock'n'roll and laying a steely foundation for the heavy metal that was to come.

Mike Bloomfield

'59 sunburst Les Paul, serial number not known, guitar 'missing in action'

Mike Bloomfield was born into a well-off Jewish family on Chicago's North Side on 28 July 1943. 'I grew up in Chicago in a Jewish and "Hillbilly" community. I heard "Black" music, didn't understand it, but loved it.'*

Bloomfield played a huge part in the American late '60s rediscovery of the Les Paul guitar. During his teenage years he had often visited blues clubs on Chicago's South Side. Initially playing a Telecaster and probably influenced by Freddie King, he soon obtained a 1954 Goldtop with P90s. Having toured England in 1966 and heard Eric Clapton, and specifically the *Beano* album, he replaced the Goldtop Les Paul with a 1959 sunburst version in the spring or summer of 1967.

What Bloomfield was tapping into here was the unique technical combination of a jazz-type guitar with a solid body 'wrongly' strung with light gauge Nashville stringing (specifically a then unusual plain third string) and Seth Lover's powerful humbuckers. The difference between Bloomfield and Clapton's approach was only in the choice of amps. Whereas Clapton and others in England favoured Marshalls, Mike stuck to home-grown Fenders, specifically the 'Super reverb'.

The original Blackface Super Reverb appeared in 1963, and was produced until 1968. The models made between 1964 and 1966 remain the most prized.

Leo Fender always strove to improve his amps and 'The Blackface's' direct ancestor was the legendary tweed Fender Bassman Amplifier from the '50s. The Fender Super Reverb was essentially the same amp as the Fender 'Concert' amp, but as the name implies it also had a built-in reverb as well as 'tremolo'. This was a popular recording amp, as it produced a very clean tone, and became a favourite with Mike Bloomfield. Ironically Jim Marshall had based his early amplifiers on Fenders.

The Super Reverb employs two 6L6 tubes in the output section, one 5AR4 rectifier tube, four 12AX7 tubes in the pre-amp section, and two 12AT7 tubes. The '65 Fender Super Reverb is a very simple amp. There are two channels (normal and vibrato), each with two inputs for each channel. Input one on each channel is made for plugging in guitars or other instruments with normal output levels. Input two on each channel has 6dB less gain than input one, and is a better choice when using an additional outboard device that boosts the gain to a higher level, such as an effects pedal. Each channel has a separate volume, treble, and bass control as well as a brightness switch. The brightness switch provides extra high-frequency response for input one on each channel. The vibrato channel also has a middle control between the treble and bass controls, which is used to adjust the middle frequency level of the vibrato channel. The vibrato channel also has a reverb knob to adjust the amount of reverb, a vibrato speed knob which adjusts the speed of the vibrato, and a vibrato intensity knob.

The one thing Mike didn't have on the amplifier was overdrive – Fender didn't yet make amplifiers with overdrive, and he also lacked any pedals to overdrive the input. So Bloomfield's sound is perhaps a little cleaner than that heard in England.

Ironically Eric Clapton claims Bloomfield also influenced *his* work, remarking that Bloomfield's 'way of thinking really shocked me the first time I met him and spoke to him. I never met anyone with so many strong convictions.'

Perhaps the most famous example of Bloomfield's Les Paul outings is the 28 May 1968 Los Angeles *Super Session* (Columbia CS-9701), where he jammed for six short hours with Blood Sweat and Tears musician Al Kooper.

What we hear here is a classic Les Paul 'blues' set-up, particularly on *Albert's Shuffle*. Here Bloomfield pays tribute to his Chicago roots and offers some classic Albert King string bends and phrasing. The sound is a little cleaner than the *Beano* album, more clearly stinging and with just the right reverb to conjure a taste of 'Chess' sessions of the '50s. The discovery of 'that classic Les Paul sound' is contrasted on the album by Stephen Stills, who plays on the other tracks and is still caught up in a 'thinner' early '60s sound – probably using a Gretsch.

Bloomfield died tragically young on 15 February 1981.

*11 May 1968 issue of *Rolling Stone*.

Eric Clapton

'60 Les Paul 'Standard', serial number not known, guitar 'missing in action'

This guitar was reported stolen during the first rehearsals for legendary super-group Cream. It remains lost.

The popular music world is full of hyperbole. However, the truth is that in April 1966 in Decca studio 2, London, this guitar, in the hands of Eric Clapton and plugged into an early Marshall '1962' combo amp, changed the sound of rock and pop music forever.

It would also revive the fortunes of the Gibson guitar company and phoenix the Les Paul from deleted obscurity to iconic status.

Eric Clapton says 'I'd seen Freddie King's album cover of *Let's Hide Away and Dance Away*, where he's playing a Goldtop,' as a result of which he went out and bought a Les Paul 'Standard' at Lew Davies' shop in the Charing Cross Road. This was as near a guitar as he could find to the P90 of Freddie King. As with practically everybody else in 1966, Eric wouldn't have known the difference between a single-coil P90 and a

humbucker. In mid-'60s Britain good American guitars were still rarities and the unpopular Les Paul model had been dropped from the Gibson catalogue in 1960. For many the electric guitar was a still a gimmick, a passing fad, and the one British guitar magazine of the time was still largely preoccupied with banjos and mandolins. The oldest production guitar available was only 15 years old and 'Vintage Guitar' meant the Stradivarius in the Ashmolean museum.

Eric described the sound of his five-year-old 'burst as 'just magnificent. I never really found one as good as that. I do miss that one.'

Prior to this he had played a Fender Telecaster and was already making a huge impact on the British club scene, initially with the Yardbirds and then with John Mayall's Bluesbreakers. 'CLAPTON IS GOD' graffiti appeared on London walls and the weekly *Melody Maker*, the bible for British musicians of the period, carried rave reviews.

Like thousands of others, the present author heard *Got To Hurry* on the B side of a Yardbirds record, where Eric was clearly striving for another sound totally different from the relatively clean guitar sounds of mid-'60s British pop. More significantly Manchester bandleader John Mayall had also heard the same disc and signed up Eric for his cult band.

Eric recording the 'Beano' album with Gus Dudgeon in April 1966.

Curious as any 15-year-old musician of the period I went down to NEMS (Brian Epstein's shop in Liverpool) and tried to buy a copy of *I'm Your Witchdoctor* by the then very obscure Bluesbreakers. They had to get the record as a special order and it took two weeks to arrive!

Like millions of others then and since, I was absolutely stunned. Eric, with help from producer-guitarist Jimmy Page, achieved a guitar sound that was wild and exciting yet under control. Suddenly the guitar was an impassioned beast, always teetering on an exciting edge of acoustic feedback and wailing distortion. This would become a new voice for the guitar, which would develop for the rest of the 20th century and beyond.

With ambitious blues producer Mike Vernon, Eric went on to record the *Beano* album. Having found his wild sound Eric was not to be tamed and gave engineer Gus Dudgeon a very difficult time, insisting that 'the sound' could only be had at full volume. In those days there were no pre-amp gain controls to adjust. If you wanted wailing distortion, it was all or nothing.

As John Mayall famously said 'our main aim was to capture our live sound on vinyl'. Eric remembers 'I wanted a bit of everything to get some kind of thickness…plus the sustain of a slide guitar.'*

Later Eric would discover that small Fender amps wound up full could achieve a similar effect (as on *Layla*), but that was the '70s and this was 1966.

Eric's amp is now known as 'The Bluesbreaker' and Jim Marshall proudly displays one in the foyer of his Milton Keynes factory. Jim told me that Eric was a frequent visitor to his little shop at 93 Uxbridge Road, Hanwell, London: 'Eric wanted a combo he could easily stick in the boot of his car…that's how the first Bluesbreaker combo came about.'

'The Bluesbreaker' was developed with Jim's right-hand man and amp designer Ken Bran. The pre-amp stage consists of three ECC83 tubes or 'valves' and the power amp is led by two 5881s/KT66s. The GL34 valve rectifier contributes greatly to the characteristic output stage compression and consequent sustain. The 12AX7/ECC83 arrangement is a phase inverter which encourages audio compression and a musical form of even harmonic distortion. The amp, rated at 30 watts, was driven into the two onboard 12in 'Greenback' Celestion speakers. These were mounted in an open-backed cabinet, which means there would be a lot more acoustic phase cancellation than that experienced in a conventional closed back 4 x 12 cabinet. Jim also employed higher 'plate' values compared to his Fender inspiration and increased the internal feedback. All these factors together add up to a very

characteristic sound. (The 1962 'Bluesbreaker' in fact has *four* ECC83s, but the fourth one just operates the tremolo.)

The other big component of the then new sound was also a happy 'accident'. Seth Lover had designed his wonderful PAF pickups to 'buck the hum', and that they did. But the two coils he wired in series also produced a slightly higher output signal than Fender single coils, and this across a broader range of frequencies than Gibson's single coil P90s.

Clapton's use of a Humbucker loaded 'Standard' into a Marshall 'Bluesbreaker' combo transformed Freddie King's clean P90 *Hide Away* into *Hideaway* – the late '60s anthem of gritty blues instrumentals. Comparing the two versions you realise Eric did much more than copy. He added a youthful passion and urgency, 'stretching out' in the more mundane boogie passages in a way that makes it his own.

We must never forget that the humble and much maligned transistor often plays a part in great 'valve' sounds. In this instance the gain at the high frequencies was boosted by Eric's introduction of a Dallas Rangemaster treble boost with circuitry based around a Mullard OC44 germanium transistor before the amp input. These 'treble boost' boxes were very popular at the time, as many '60s British amps sounded a bit bland 'straight off the shelf'.

The Rangemaster overloaded the front end of Jim Marshall's amp and that creamy distortion was then passed on to the power amp stage rectified and compressed.

In 1966 the characteristic sound of the guitar in 'white boys' blues' had been defined. The Les Paul was king and Stratocasters were almost being given away (until Jimi Hendrix fortunately made an impact). Here's a typical story. Kim Simmonds of The Savoy Blues Band heard The Bluesbreakers live at The Flamingo, Soho, London, in 1966:

'Clapton was playing a Gibson Les Paul though a strange amplifier…a Marshall amplifier it turned out. Jack Bruce was on bass and the band rocked. Eric's guitar sound and style was a combination of all the American guitarists I was then listening to (and trying to copy) – BB King, Steve Cropper, Otis Rush and Lonnie Mack – all put together by an Englishman the size of me. I told him how good he was, walked home, sold my Fender and bought a Gibson!'*

Rock had yet to be invented but the stage was set, and Jimmy Page was there at the beginning. I met him at the time in Denmark Street and he told me he was thinking of forming his own band. Led Zeppelin was conceived in 1966, with the sound of a cranked-up Les Paul and overdriven Marshall ringing in our ears.

Mojo magazine, May 1988.

Peter Green

'Pious bird of good omen'

'59 Les Paul serial number 9 2038

■ Scene-set: *Interior a seedy pub in '60s swinging London – The Nag's Head, Battersea, a crowded upstairs room known for tonight as 'The Blue Horizon Club':*
It's 1968 and I'm 17 years old. Legally speaking I shouldn't be in a pub, but I've been working as a musician in pubs and clubs since I was 11 so I'm well practised at looking tall!

The reason I've left my native Liverpool is standing three feet away on the tiny stage. Peter Green has just played a blistering blues opener on his

Peter Green and John McVie
circa 1967.

' He has the sweetest tone I ever heard. He's the only one who gave me the cold sweats. '

BB King

'59 Sunburst. In the process he's blown up his shiny new Orange amplifier. Earlier in the day I'd seen him pick this amp up new in a music store in 'Tin Pan Alley' – Denmark Street W1. Peter Green is a little miffed.

A roadie lumbers on stage with a backup amp, a shredded VOX AC 30. I am mortified. I know the AC30, I have three back home at my dad's house in Liverpool – the amp is a great little workhorse, especially for cleanish Shadows' sounds and Duane Eddy twang – but the blues? The blues is the *Beano* album and beat-up Marshalls – we *all* know that. I feel this isn't going to work.

Peter Green, however, is unfazed as he plugs in, winds up the volume and *3, 4... Love That Burns.* I'm astonished because he sounds exactly like he always does. The magic isn't in the valves, or transformers or blue speakers; it's in his head and finds its way to his fingers. A little alchemy *is* added to the mix by Peter's now famous phase-inverted pickup; it gives a characteristic hollow vocal quality to his impeccable phrasing. But the real magic is Peter Green.

The band finish the set and I and the hundred or so others in the room are left astonished – this guy is a genius and soon even BB King is saying so.

Before he leaves the stage Peter announces the band's new single, which is then played on the appalling house PA. It's a weird, almost-Shadows like tune with a lot of distorted bass on this poor PA system – Peter mumbled something about a 'Pious Bird of Good Omen'. Next week it's number one in the charts and you couldn't see Peter Green in a pub for ten bob any more. The single was *Albatross*.

■ *Cut to the present:*
The reason behind this nostalgia is to get over what I feel is the most important aspect of the vintage Les Paul mythology. Peter Green was *happy* playing that particular guitar – it perhaps inspired him, but if needs be he could have played almost as well on his previous guitar, a Harmony Meteor. I'm sure the most important component in the sound chain is the musician.

For the record these are two theories about the sound of the '59 Les Paul 'Greeny':

■ Peter removed one pickup from the guitar as a tribute to his hero Eric Clapton, who only seemed to need one pickup! He later put one of the pickups back in the guitar the wrong way round. He mentioned this himself in a recent interview.
■ The rest of the likely truth is documented in the 'Greeny' case study (*see page 148*).

So given that most of Peter Green's sound is in his musicianship, what can we learn specifically about the sound of those fantastic early records? I interviewed the producer Mike Vernon:

'The first Mac album was recorded at CBS Studio, New Bond Street, London, with the previous demos recorded at Decca No 2 and 3 studios, also in London. The engineer was usually Mike Ross. There *were* some overdubs but a lot of that first album was recorded all at once. Peter preferred to record the vocals and guitar simultaneously live, but there were occasional overdubs. He would sing and then overdub guitar. The multi-track was an eight-track Studer. Peter played all the guitar parts on *Albatross*, including the slide solo.'

Mike had this to say about his approach to producing those legendary sessions: 'I have always maintained that a producer should be more like an extra member of the band and not stand alone giving orders or dishing out opinions left, right and centre. I tried that a couple of times and it didn't work! Be understanding and always do your best to be helpful. If someone in the band has an idea, hear it out. If it turns out to be a "no go" then that's the way it will go – invariably. When you feel the need to make an observation or ask for another take or a change in the routine or solo or whatever, don't be scared to say your piece – do it politely and with respect, and in that way build a strong working relationship with the band. Try to be the catalyst for the end result. Oh yes, and never looked bored – they'll twig – and then you're out! But perhaps above all, be patient, and with a following wind and a sense of humour everything should go swimmingly.'

All of the above follows the regular pattern of '60s and '70s recording and performing. The gear was all solid, reliable engineering developed in the '30s and '40s. Good valve and ribbon microphones sensibly placed, valve-based desks and Swiss engineering on the analogue tape machines. The *magic* is in the players and their interaction with the moment.

As Peter Green says himself 'That '59 was no magic stick.' It was a well set up, accidentally wired out-of-phase, well-made '59 burst.

■ **For the record, Peter Green amplification**
AMPS Vox AC100 and 2 x Vox T60 15in and 12in bass cabs Marshalls. MatAmp 20 watt Series 2000 (MatAmp) GT120. Fender Dual Showman Reverb head with pair of 15in speakers. As observed above, Fleetwood Mac were also an early customer for Orange amps.

Gary Moore

1959 Les Paul 'Standard', serial no not known

For many years Gary Moore famously owned 'Greeny', the 1959 'Standard' which he unbelievably bought from British blues genius Peter Green for £120. This is the guitar on *Blues for Greeny*, the 1995 project that was Gary's tribute to his hero. For more on this guitar see the Peter Green 'key player' section on page 148. When he played Peter Green material, Gary seemed to naturally return to this 'quirky out-of-phase guitar'.

However, Gary has many other Les Pauls, including *another* '59 'Standard'.

For his historic appearance at the Montreux Festival, 7 July 1990, as part of the 'Still Got The Blues' tour, Gary played this other guitar. The Montreux guitar is without pickup covers, has non-zebra bobbins and has 'original' tulip machine head pegs.

('Greeny' currently has Grover machine heads and has the pickup covers 'ON'.)

For this outing Gary seems to have wanted a natural full-throated Les Paul sound, mainly using the neck pickup.

His favourite amplification at this time consisted of a Marshall '1962' Mk I of circa 1965 and a Super Tremolo 2 x 12in combo. The grill cloth on this amp had been changed at some point, and also the output transformer, which is ironically from a VOX AC30. A Tube Screamer or Guv'nor pedal usually provides Gary some extra drive into the front end.

The Ibanez Tube Screamer is a relatively subtle analogue overdrive device invented by Ibanez's S. Tamura, which is noted for its intelligent 'soft clipping'. This utilises a JRC4558D 1980 chip employed throughout the life of the TS-808. There is another 4558 chip, the TL4558P, sometimes employed as an alternative. In AB tests there is little difference between the chips, although the JRC gives the strongest classic tube screamer sound – a sweet vocal midrange*. Interestingly Stevie Ray Vaughan also used this same unit for many of his classic recordings when a subtle overdrive was needed.

The Guv'nor pedal in its first classic '80s incarnation is dedicated to the venerable Jim Marshall – 'the father of loud'. Like the Ibanez this is an overdrive pedal capable of subtle overload with a sophisticated EQ control to tailor the guitar output before the amp.

For the first solo of the Montreux gigs, *Still Got The Blues*, Gary demonstrates what the Les Paul does best, providing a wonderful gutsy sustain with which Gary weaves his own magic. His brilliant melodic sense means he can simply state the tune, sometimes alternating octaves, but always providing the listener with a clear roadmap through his improvised decorations.

For the second solo Gary starts with another statement of the melody, this time adding more and wider vibrato to the Les Paul's wonderful sustain and exploiting the clarity the guitar maintains even in the bottom octave. Gradually he introduces more chromatic passing notes using the cutaway to the full to reach the 22nd fret and by 'bending' the notes reaching beyond that.

What is really impressive, however, is how the guitar still retains its tone and character as Gary reduces the dynamic to a melodic whisper for a final chorus and thumb-picked final arpeggios.

It's all in the fingers!

* Thanks to analogman.com for this research

Mick Taylor

'59 Les Paul 'Standard', serial no not known

■ *1967 'The British Blues Boom', London, upstairs in a Chalk Farm Pub:*
'The University of Mayall' certainly schooled some guitar players. By 1967 Eric Clapton had graduated to form Cream and Peter Green to Fleetwood Mac. On stage today at this humble pub there was no guitarist in sight. An 18-year-old Mick Taylor, clearly overwhelmed by his natural shyness and the size of the acts he had to follow, remained hidden behind a huge Marshall Stack. Jimi Hendrix was in town, Eric Clapton was jamming with Stevie Winwood and planning a tour, Jimmy Page was doing sessions and jamming with rock royalty.

Pity, then, Mick Taylor, glimpsed occasionally with a '59 Les Paul. At least he'd found the right guitar. The pub gig went OK, Mayall took the weight off Mick's shoulders, played and sang, even played his weird hybrid nine-string guitar. We all went home from the gig a little confused, but when Mick *had* played he had 'the sound', and soon the albums appeared that showed he'd found his feet.

Mick soon went on to lift The Rolling Stones from fading pop star mediocrity to a new level of blues-based credibility. His Les Paul went with him.

■ *Cut forward to 2003:*
Incredibly, John Mayall is celebrating his 70th birthday in my hometown of Liverpool, bringing together the great guitarists of The Bluesbreakers.

Mick Taylor's spot is especially interesting, as together with Buddy Whittington we are treated to both forms of classic blues guitar 'hardware', a Strat and a Les Paul onstage together, Buddy with a wonderful '50s-style Sunburst Stratalike made by Scott Lentz and Mick with a fabulous Les Paul 'burst. The tune is *Blues For The Lost Days*:

Lookin' back through the years
Like I got myself a time machine

A 'blues whisper' from the venerable John Mayall nudges Mick off to a tentative answering phrase start – an unusual fingerstyle on the 'burst. The lyrics pour out nostalgia for the Flamingo club and 'Hard Roads' of old. It's all a bit too 'easy'. The mighty Hammond sizzles and the Fender bass growls, the drummer drives and syncopates…it's familiar and muddy water.

Then Buddy Whittington throws a lyrical Stratotastic punch straight from the heart of Otis Rush; clean as mountain air. Mick comes back with that *other* blues voice, the warm rush of maple and mahogany, PAFs and wire – the Bluesbreaker fit to burst. Buddy comes back all Robert Cray and a Buddy Guy chaser, straight up no water. A bit of BB King understatement *on a Strat!* And Buddy literally takes off.

This is one of those moments improvising musicians live for: Liverpool! John Mayall and Mick Taylor, Eric Clapton in the wings, the ghost of 'a crumpled Beano' drifting through the blue lights and shadow. Everybody feels the bare wires as Buddy soars through every blues he has ever lived.

'*Electricity!* Cold Steel and bare wire', a turnaround and a knowing smile.

Mick picks up the glove and gently talks back, a beautiful shorter scale stop tail vibrato, easing into his stride. The 'burst has that distinctive reedy voice, all tobacco and rye, back pickup and bare fingers. Somewhere a valve is gently clipping; even harmonics sing.

Mick plays across the time, skipping beats and taking another soaring chorus. A repeated note BB King stammer, a Hendrix hammer on and Wah, and proceedings move forward to '69.

For a last verse call and response Mick shows how a 'burst works just fine with a bottleneck too.

The John Mayall 70th beano wouldn't be right without a little 'Sunburst'.

A DVD treat worth checking out.

■ **Mick's amplification**
With John Mayall back in the '60s this was Marshall 100 watt stacks and half-stacks with occasional Marshall 50 watt stacks and half-stacks. Latterly an Ampeg VT-40 sometimes modified with 6550 power tubes (heard on the *Joe Henry* album), also an Ampeg VT-22, Ampeg GU-35 (in the studio and backstage with The Stones), Ampeg B-15 or B-25 Portaflex bass amp, Fender Twin Reverbs, Marshall 2 x 12in combo, a Mesa Boogie (model unknown, as used on the '79 solo album), a 'Pignose', a Roland JC120 (as used on the '79 solo album) and a MusicMan (for Bob Dylan's '84 summer tour).

Jimmy Page

Various Les Paul 'bursts and Black Beauties

In the early days Jimmy was often seen with a three-pickup Custom 'Black Beauty'. Since then he's been seen predominantly with a couple of 'bursts which have evolved into the production Gibson 'Signature' guitar.

Crucially the first eight bars of *Led Zeppelin II* mark a turning point in the evolution of 'Classic Rock': Eric Clapton with Cream, Jeff Beck with The Yardbirds, Mike Bloomfield and a dozen West Coast USA pioneers had set the fuse, many of them playing Les Paul guitars. Blues-based riffs and 12-bar I/IV/V harmonic structures were prevalent.

However, when the simple anthemic three-note riff of *Whole*

Lotta Love seismically disturbed the diamond stylus in seven million vinyl grooves there was no going back. The fusion of '50s rock'n'roll, Chicago blues, Celtic folk and a little Hendrix Voodoo created a Marshall-amplified raptor that would change popular music forever.

Ironically all this happened on a diminutive solid-bodied jazz guitar designed for Tuxedo-clad musicians in Las Vegas lounges. From now on the true home of the Les Paul guitar was centre stage 'stadium rock'.

At the time of the first Led Zeppelin album Jimmy Page had used both a '58 Fender Telecaster and a Les Paul 'Black Beauty'

with three humbuckers and a Bigsby vibrato (which was sadly stolen in 1970).

By the recording of the second album (*Led Zeppelin II*) Jimmy had moved to the classic Les Paul 'Standards' and various Marshall stacks.

■ Jimmy Page Les Pauls

Jimmy's Les Pauls deserve special mention for the electronic versatility he had built into the guitars *without* changing the classic aesthetics. Many guitars in the '70s suffered major cosmetic surgery, which usually detracted from their classic design – but Jimmy had the good sense to leave the basic guitar alone.

For three decades he has mainly used two Les Pauls:

■ A sunburst-finished '59 'Standard'. This has been modified with a shaved neck (not by Page) and the addition of push/pull pots to coil split the humbuckers *(see page 92)*.

■ A '58 'Standard', bought from Joe Walsh and very similar in appearance to the above, leading to confusion over which is which (this information from Page's guitar tech). It was modified as per the '59 model but with the addition of two switches under the pickguard, one for series/parallel switching, the other a phase reversal switch. This guitar Roger Giffin copied at Gibson's Custom Shop, and that specification eventually became Jimmy's 'Signature' Les Paul series model. On the 'Signature' guitars the series/parallel and phase switches became push/pull pots and the guitar has a compound radius fingerboard.

■ Jimmy's amps

Marshall SLP-1959 100-watt amp modified with KT-88 tubes, for increased output. He has also used Vox, Hiwatt, Fender Super reverbs and Orange amps.

■ Effects

A Roger Mayer fuzz box, Sola Sound Tonebender, Vox Cry Baby Wah, Maestro Echoplex, MXR Phase 90, MXR Blue Box.

■ Picks

Herco Flex 75.

■ Strings

Electric: Ernie Ball Super Slinky. Acoustic: Ernie Ball Earthwoods. Jimmy also famously uses a battered violin bow to further attack his Gibsons.

Source: Mikesguitarsite.co.uk

Jimmy Page 'Signature Model'

Recently Gibson's Custom, Art & Historic division have introduced a Jimmy Page 'Signature' Les Paul model which replicates the unique neck shape and custom electronics of the '58 sunburst Gibson Les Paul (the Joe Walsh guitar). The neck of Page's guitar is thick at the nut and at the neck heel, like a typical late '50s Les Paul, but it tapers to a super-slim depth in the middle (like his modified '59). This has the push/pull pots in the volume control that reverses the phase, and the original tuners are replaced by sealed, 'gold'-plated Grovers to achieve the tuning stability and sensitivity of the Les Paul 'Custom' he had first played with Led Zeppelin.

The 'Signature' model comes equipped with Jimmy Page custom BurstBuckers (a hot version of the PAF). It also features a special Page 'burst finish, and the authentic look was further enhanced on 150 limited edition Jimmy Page Les Pauls with custom ageing by renowned luthier Tom Murphy. This was followed by an unlimited run with the Custom 'Authentic' treatment.

■ Body

Top wood: Carved figured maple
Back wood: Solid mahogany
Binding: Single-ply cream on top
Available left-handed: No
Finish colours: Page 'Burst, aged by Tom Murphy

■ Neck

Neck construction: One-piece mahogany with long neck tenon
Fingerboard wood: 22-fret rosewood
Inlays: Vintage trapezoid (accurate shape and colour)
Binding: Single-ply cream
Profile: Jimmy Page custom
Scale length/Nut width: 24¾in/1 11/16in
Strings: Vintage reissue .010–.046

■ Electronics and hardware

Pickups: Jimmy Page custom BurstBuckers
Controls: Two volume, two tone, three-way switch, push/pull pot for series/parallel switching
Hardware colour: Aged nickel and gold
Bridge/Tailpiece: ABR-1/Lightweight aluminium
Tuner style: Kidney bean

Mark Knopfler

'84 Les Paul 'burst reissue serial no 90006

Ironically the same man who revived the Stratocaster's fortunes in the early '80s would turn to Les Paul's guitar for his most celebrated album, *Brothers in Arms*. The Les Paul contributes the signature rock grunt to *Money For Nothing* and a sweet understated solo to the title track.

For *Money For Nothing* Mark applied his very individual fingerpicking style to a rock riff played on a then new Gibson Les Paul reissue. The other factors in play included an unusual use of a wah pedal as a frequency filter.

Mark's guitar tech Ron Eve told me: 'The half-cocked wah on *Money For Nothing* was a Cry Baby we fiddled with while he played the riff (THAT riff) until he liked it. On tour we got Pete Cornish to build one into a rack with a screwdriver-controlled pot that we adjusted to match the sound.

'Mark's Les Paul is a beauty, even though it's a reissue. I rewired the pickups so that the central position selector combined them "out of phase". This trick was shown to me by a guitar luthier in London a long time ago – Sam Lee – who did it accidentally on Peter Green's Les Paul. If you listen closely to the early Fleetwood Mac albums you can hear the type of sound made *(see page 148 for more on this)*. On *Brothers in Arms* his Les Paul was used through a Marshall JTM45 amp head (which was mine at the time!) and Marshall cab with four EVs.'

Producer Neil Dorfsman also used some interesting recording gear at the recording venue – George Martin's Air Montserrat Studio. (He also disagrees over the kind of amp Mark used):

'I was stunned when we got there because the studio was tiny. Still, it had a beautiful old Neve 8078, which I think was the best-sounding board Neve ever made, and that was the sound of the records that came out of there. Shortly after *Brothers In Arms* they replaced it with an SSL, and I thought that was a huge mistake.

'It was pretty torturous…It was a good-sounding studio, but the main room itself was nothing to write home about. The sound of that studio was the desk. Still, we crowded everybody in there, recording with at least three or four guys on every tune, while I built little rooms out of gobos and baffles and blankets. The reason for going to Montserrat was that it was a great place to hang out and it was very relaxed, so you could focus on what you were doing. And the board was so good that anything you put through it just sounded great. However, you wouldn't go there to get an ambient room recording.

'Generally, when I record I like to record close and have some ambient stuff as well – some distant mikes on guitars, the drums, whatever – but you really couldn't do that there. Everything had to be close-miked and quite heavily baffled, which was not a style I liked. I'd grown up working at the Power Station, which had a really, really large room with a really big isolation room, so you could isolate everything but still have ambience on all the instruments. As a result it was very difficult for me to get my head around the situation in Montserrat – a very '70s style of recording; close-miked, dead, and you would leave it to the mix to create ambience. I didn't enjoy that part of it, but because the board sounded so good I still loved working there, despite the acoustics of the room.

'I remember Mark's Les Paul going through a Laney amp [!], and that was the sound of *Money For Nothing*. We were actually going for a sort of ZZ Top sound, but what we ended up getting was kind of an accident.

'Mark would be in the control room and we'd run a lead out to the main area, and I remember getting a channel set up to monitor, heading out to the room to move the mikes around Mark's guitar. Tech Ron Eve was on the talkback and telling me not to touch anything because it sounded amazing as it was.

'One mike was pointing down at the floor, another was not quite on the speaker, another was somewhere else, and it wasn't how I would want to set things up … it was probably just left from the night before, when I'd been preparing things for the next day and had not really finished the set-up. Nevertheless, whether it was the phase of the mikes or the out-of-phaseness, what we heard was exactly what ended up on the record. There was no additional processing on that tune during the mix.

'Later on, a lot of people asked me how I got the sound on the record, but it was just one of those happy accidents that have not happened to me very often. I don't know if something was broken, but we could not recreate that sound again. All I know is it was the sound of Mark playing, using his fingers instead of a pick, together with the Laney amp. It felt and sounded so good that I just had him do five or six passes and later comped something together and wound up using a couple of the passes in the final mix, putting a double in at certain

points even though that wasn't something he normally did.'

About two months had been spent at AIR Montserrat, as well as a couple of weeks at the Power Station for additional overdubs using an SSL E-series desk together with the Sony 24-track digital recorder.

'Thanks to Mark, that album was among the first to be recorded on a Sony 24-track digital tape machine,' explains Neil. 'One of the things that I totally respected about him was his interest in technology as a means of improving his music. He was always willing to spend on high-quality equipment, and I actually remember the night he made the decision to try digital.

'We were working on *Love Over Gold* at the Power Station, and we spent a really long time getting the piano sound for a song called *Private Investigations*. We were so impressed with the result that we played it back several times for people to hear, but every time we played it back the sound lost something. I can recall the expression on Mark's face: dismay and a look of "We've got to do something about this. The sound is going to wear out." It was at that point the light bulb went on in his head and in my head that we had to work in another way, and digital seemed to be the answer.

'But was it the answer? After all, the sound of those early 16-bit digital machines was nothing compared to that of the current generation.

'However, the Sony 24-track that we used for the entire *Brothers in Arms* album was a different story. I loved it from the very beginning, I thought it was great.

'I'd never liked the way analogue tape changed the sound – I was always disappointed with what was played back right after recording. I didn't like the way it changed the bottom end and softened things. A lot of people do like that, but I never did. And when people asked me, after *Brothers in Arms* came out, whether I'd changed my miking technique or style of recording to accommodate digital, I told them I'd done exactly the same things that I'd done with analogue, but without having to worry about adding extra top end because it would degenerate.'

What makes that great riff in the end is Mark's idiosyncratic and distinctive phrasing – never quite repeating himself, always instinctively finding a slightly different take on a killer riff.

The album is also distinguished by some very mellow and heartfelt improvising on the title track – also played on the same Les Paul. It's in the head and the heart, and with practice finds its way to the fingers. And interestingly not an authentic vintage guitar in sight! So some of the 'burst's most popular moments came from a wonderfully set up reproduction.

Now there's a thought to ponder.

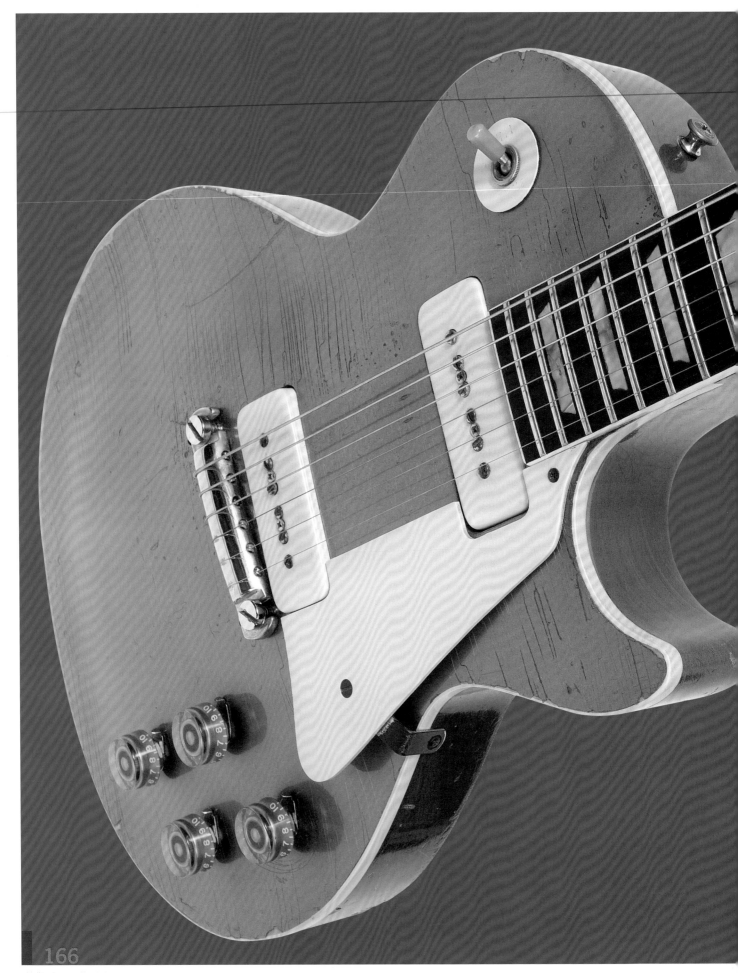

Appendices, glossary and contacts

Some further notes on guitar design, guitar tuning, screw sizes and serial numbers.

LEFT Gold Top '53

RIGHT Gold Top '53

Les Paul design concepts

Introduced in 1952 for $210 and advertised as 'Designed by Les Paul produced by Gibson', in many ways the Les Paul guitar is an arch top jazz guitar that lacks a hollow cavity (Pete Frampton models aside).

This may seem elementary but this fundamental seems to underpin the guitar's whole design philosophy. Les Paul himself had done his best work on Gibson and Epiphone archtops that had been radically modified to eliminate the problems associated with both acoustic feedback and the cancellation issues arising from a moving pickup tracking a moving string. That Gibson should want their first solid-body guitar to follow in its own archtop tradition is logical and suits the mood of 1952, when Leo Fender's 'canoe paddle' was still a point of derision amongst traditional luthiers.

The body laminate sandwich of mahogany and maple had been arrived at following considerable experimentation. Maple apparently sustained too long (which seems incredible given the subsequent history of the guitar) and so the mahogany mix became the 'regular' arrangement. The fabulous maple flame remained hidden beneath the gold top or thick black nitro cellulose lacquer until '57 and nobody liked it enough then to sustain the guitar in production.

The rest of the Les Paul is pretty stock Gibson 1950s – the post-war plastics for knobs and bindings, Kluson machines, mahogany neck and rosewood fingerboard et al. Even the P90 pickups had been tried on archtops.

As the guitar moved away from its archtop roots, ditching its trapeze tailpiece, trying a brief excursion into experimental 'alnico V' pickups, acquiring a Tune-O-Matic and Seth Lover's more powerful humbucker, it became a classic, but also a fashion victim. By this time an electric guitar preferably needed to be a red object that screamed of a space age future. Sunburst finishes and violin contours were not the fashion statement of 1960.

The distinctive voice of the Les Paul had to wait another six years for a new wave of sustain-seeking, Blues-based guitarists who liked the way a humbucker could overdrive the front end of a 'class A' thermionic tube amplifier.

■ Appendix 2
Tempered tuning – the great compromise

'Equal temperament' is the name given to a system of dividing the chromatic scale into 12 exactly equal half-steps. This is a compromise, but does allow us to play reasonably in tune in all keys and to modulate between keys during a performance.

Guitarists must learn to understand and accept equal temperament. (You might be interested to know that to approximate 'pure' chords in all forms would require about three dozen frets within the octave.) The system of equal temperament reduces the required fret number to 12. A workable compromise.

Many guitarists are frustrated in their attempts to tune the guitar to pure chords (free of perceived 'beats'). These players have very sensitive ears that prefer 'pure' intervals and reject the mandatory equal temperament. They tune their guitar beautifully pure on one chord, only to discover that the next chord form is unacceptable. In too many instances they assume that there must be a flaw in the workmanship on the fingerboard. However, the problem is not in the construction of the guitar. Rather it is one of 'pure' or 'mean tone' tuning versus equal temperament.

A 'mean tone' fretted guitar would in fact only sound acceptably in tune in about three keys, so from the 18th century onwards we've learned to live with the compromise of equal temperament. Prior to this lutes and early guitars often had movable 'gut' frets which were tempered to the key of the piece to be performed. This system works fine until the piece modulates into a different key. The modern North Indian sitar still retains movable frets and the player tempers his frets according to the raga he is about to perform. Indian music, however, never modulates.

As practical working guitarists we must accept the equal tempered compromise, because the guitar is an instrument of fixed pitch and the strings must be tuned to tempered intervals, not 'pure'.

■ Appendix 3
Potentiometer codes

As the value of vintage Les Pauls continues to escalate collectors are looking for guidance on authenticity. 'Pot codes' are one form of cross-reference, as this fairly sophisticated system of numbering employed on 1950s and '60s American electronic components can offer valuable dating clues. Beware, however, that this may give rise to a mini industry in fake pots!

I'm grateful to Dave Gregory for introducing me to pot codes and to The Vintage Guitar Gallery for the following data.

Pot codes have the following configurations: MMMYWW or MMMYYWW. The first three digits indicate the maker of the pot.

Among the most common are the following:

Code	Maker
106	Allen-Bradley Corporation
134	Centralab
137	CTS (Chicago Telephone Supply)
140	Clarostat
220	Jensen
304	Stackpole
328	Utah/Oxford
381	Bourns Networks
465	Oxford

The fourth digit in a six-digit code corresponds to the last digit of the year of manufacture. Pot makers used a six-digit code prior to 1961 and a seven-digit code from 1961 onwards. Some other companies, however, continued with a six-digit code.

The fourth and fifth digits in a seven-digit code correspond to the last two digits of the year of manufacture.

The final two digits in a six-digit code or a seven-digit code correspond to the week of the year in which the pot was made. Note: A series of numbers greater than 53 cannot be a week dating code as it would be higher than the number of weeks in a year.

■ **Appendix 4**
Replacement screw sizes

Luthier John Diggins has encountered a lot of Les Pauls and offers the following guidance:

■ Machine heads – No. 2 roundhead Phillips (this would have been No. 3 on the early models).
■ Truss rod cover – No. 3 roundhead Phillips.
■ Strap buttons – No. 6 raised countersunk Phillips.
■ Pick-guard body fixings – No. 3 raised countersunk Phillips.
■ Pick-guard bracket fixing – 6 UNC flat countersunk Phillips.
■ Pickup height adjustment screws – 3 UNC roundhead Phillips (slotted on the early models).
■ Pickup surround screws – No. 2 flat countersunk Phillips.
■ Toggle switch cap thread – 8 UNC.
■ Jack plate screws – No. 3 raised countersunk Phillips.
■ Switch and electronics back plate screws – No. 3 raised countersunk Phillips.
■ Bridge height adjustment studs – 6 UNC.
■ Tailpiece anchor posts – 5/16 UNF.

■ **Appendix 5**
Comparative output levels

All figures relate to the pickup outputs with all tone and volume controls set to maximum.

I used an averaged sample of my own plectrum downstroke. All the guitars except the '53 (which was tested on a small Fender combo) were amplified by the same Fender Hot Rod Deluxe with an AKG cardiod microphone placed six inches from the centre of the loudspeaker cone. Sound desk settings and amplifier settings were consistent EQ Flat etc. The measurements were done using a BBC spec PPM meter 'O' level = .775 volts.

Pickup outputs
Reference 'O' level = −18dBV.

1977 'Deluxe' Goldtop (Epiphone USA Mini-humbuckers)
■ −18dBV both pickups were equal and summed at the same level in the middle pickup selector position.

Custom '57 reissues
■ −20dB both pickups summed (mid pos), *ie* two dB quieter than
■ −18dB bridge pickup alone.
■ −20dB neck pickup alone (which suggests some phase cancellation of the pickup outputs output when combined – a typical characteristic of the 'Les Paul' sound).

NB Both our 'Black Beauties' showed near identical outputs despite the neck pickup on the non-Bigsby guitar being set slightly further from the strings.

Gibson USA 'Standard' 2006
■ −20dB all pickup combinations.

Gibson USA 'Quilt Top' '59 neck
■ −20dB both pickups summed.
■ −18dB bridge pickup alone.
■ −20dB neck pickup alone.

NB The pickups on this guitar were factory set considerably further from the strings than most of the other guitars (almost flush with the surrounds), suggesting they have more output in reserve?

Customised Epiphone 'Standard'

NB This budget guitar was retro fitted with Seymour Duncan 'jazz' pickups as part of this Haynes project. These were also wired for coil tapping, enabling single coil or humbucking modes. It also had a new bone nut, a fret polish and a good general set-up prior to these tests. Despite its 'fake' top and budget appointments this *is* a real 'Les Paul', as Lester Polfus says in the guitar's associated advertising. If Lester were playing it you would probably not detect any significant difference in sound as compared to his 'Artist' Gibsons – however, I'm sure he *feels* better playing the latter and this is, I'm sure, a very significant factor in a player's subsequent artistic performance.

On a technical note the 'humbucking' principle applied during these tests – in single coil mode my PC introduced a high pitch whine to the guitar's sound when the two objects were closer together than 1m. This whine disappeared completely in 'humbucking' mode.

Humbucking mode:
- –21dB both pickups summed.
- –21dB bridge pickup alone.
- –19dB neck pickup alone.

Single coil mode:
- –23 dB both pickups summed.
- –22 dB bridge pickup alone.
- –22 dB neck pickup alone.

Single coil 'twang' and only a dB or two less drive – very useful.

Epiphone 'Special' 2
- –18dB both pickups summed.
- –18dB bridge pickup alone.
- –18dB neck pickup alone.

NB On this guitar the bridge pickup was factory set very close to the strings, producing a strident aggressive sound – very suitable for punk or modern metal aspirations. This not a polite guitar but finds great favour with many young students including my own pupil, 'Voodoo Chile' Michael Adams (then aged nine). The 'uncanned' open Zebra coils sound best with lots of pre-amp drive and have a natural microphonic tendency, which can be very effective in certain musical contexts.

Other subjective observations

1. In this side by side test the '60 neck Gibson 'Standard' with its BurstBuckers had a rawer, edgier sound than the slightly more refined 'Black Beauties'. However, there are many other factors to consider here – solid mahogany versus maple cap, slimmer neck, Bigsby, weight, etc.

2. Note the '77 Goldtop produces *more* output despite its mini humbuckers, not less!

3. The subjectively 'loudest' guitar was the cheapest – the Special 2. Size is not everything, however!

Gibson HD6X PRO
- –18dB both pickups summed.
- –18dB bridge pickup alone.
- –18dB neck pickup alone.

NB The 'Digital' output is also nominally '0' level into a line input.

Epiphone '56 Goldtop reissue – P90s, single coil
- –21dB both pickups summed.
- –20dB bridge pickup alone.
- –20dB neck pickup alone.

Gibson Peter Frampton Custom Shop
- –18dB all modes.

Gibson '53 Goldtop
- –18dB all modes.

What I find remarkable is the consistency of measured output level on these guitars (all within the 3dB window regarded as the smallest discernible subjective level change), this despite very different pickups – clearly Gibson has a policy in this area. What does differ is 'perceived' *loudness* – a subjective judgement, nevertheless well documented, which has much to do with frequency range and harmonic content – what we might generally term 'tone'.

Guitar expert Dave Hunter has observed: 'A close examination of an original Gibson PAF pickup of 1957–'62 (as reproduced in Gibson's Burstbucker or '57 Classic) reveals that they don't have DC resistance readings in the 10k to 12k ohms range like high-gain humbuckers, but hover down in the 6.5k to 7.5k range, no hotter than plenty of singlecoil pickups. The same relative "coolness" applies to vintage P-90s when compared to many modern replacements inspired by that classic Gibson singlecoil (and note that a P-90 and a PAF humbucker really have very similar outputs, even though they sound quite different).'

■ Appendix 6
Headstock angles

All the guitars made available had a headstock angle of a nominal 16.5°–17°.

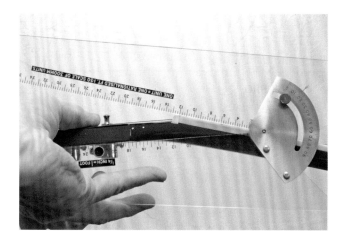

Gibson used this pitch consistently until late 1965. Some guitars were then produced with a lesser 14° pitch. This change coincides with the introduction of the reinforcing volute at the back of the headstock/neck. Both the volute and the 14° pitch were unpopular and were soon discontinued.

■ Appendix 7
Serial numbers
Source: Gibson.com.

In 1977 Gibson introduced the serialisation method still in use today. This system utilises an impressed eight-digit numbering scheme that covers both serialising and dating functions. The pattern is YDDDYPPP, where YY is the production year, DDD is the day of the year, and PPP is the plant designation and/or instrument rank.

Since 1989 acoustic guitars built at the Bozeman, Montana, facility are ranked from 001 to 499, while electric guitars built at the Gibson USA plant in Nashville are ranked from 500 to 999. Prior to 1984 the numbers 001–499 show Kalamazoo production while 500–999 show Nashville production. The serial numbers from the Custom, Art, and Historic division vary depending on the line. The historic reissue guitars feature historically accurate serial numbers.

70108276 would therefore be an instrument produced on 10 January 1978 in Kalamazoo, and would be the 276th instrument stamped that day.

82765501 would be an instrument produced on 3 October 1985 in Nashville, and would be the first instrument stamped that day.

For more details on Gibson serialisation prior to 1977 and historical product specs view the Gibson.com website, where they offer a PDF file.

Epiphone Les Pauls
According to Gibson the first Epiphone Les Pauls were manufactured in Korea in 1989.

Most regular production models since 1993, and many '80s and early '90s serial numbers, may follow a similar scheme to Gibson, but may not include a factory ID code. The coding pattern is FYYMMRRRR, where F is the factory code (which can be one or two letters), YY is the year of manufacture (this might be just one digit for '90s models), MM is the month of manufacture and R is the ranking number (this may be more or less digits, and is not necessarily indicative of the total units produced). An example would be S02021234, issued in February 2002.

Another code used on some current Epiphone models is FYYMRRRR, where F is the factory code, YY the year of manufacture, M a letter code corresponding to the month (A = January, B = February, etc) and RRRR is the ranking number. An example would be R03D0263, issued in April 2003.

Epiphone Elite/Elitist models use the pattern FYSSSS, where F is the factory code (this will be an 'F' or 'T'), Y the year of manufacture (2 = 2002, 3 = 2003, etc) and SSSS the sequential serial number. For example, T41234 would be a 2004 Elitist model.

According to *Gruhn's Guide to Vintage Guitars*: 'Almost all foreign-made Epiphones from 1970 to the mid 1990s were made in Japan or Korea. Many have a 7-digit serial number for which no list is available. Beginning in the late 1980s, some examples have a number in which the first digit corresponds to the last digit of the year, or the first two digits correspond to the last two digits of the year. In the 1990s, some models have a number beginning with a letter, signifying the manufacturing facility, followed by a digit corresponding with the last digit of the year. Recently, guitars have a factory letter code (or two), followed by the last two digits of the year of manufacture and the month of manufacture.'

■ Appendix 8
Other Les Paul guitars

This volume has of necessity largely confined itself to the 'classic' Les Paul guitar, though the 'Les Paul' designation has appeared on several radically different models.

As early as 1954 Gibson introduced a 'Junior' as a student model. This lacked the classic carved top and any binding.

In 1960 as the popularity of 'Sunburst', 'Goldtop' and 'Black Beauty' coloured archtop guitars drastically diminished Gibson started to apply the Les Paul signature to a radical new design that eventually came to be known as the 'SG'.

These distinct guitars merit their own volumes.

Even within the confines of the classic Les Paul there have been many divergences, notably an unsuccessful hollow-bodied model and several Les Paul 'lites', notably the female-targeted 'Vixen' and 'Goddess' models – stripped down to basics and heavily weight relieved.

The Les Paul 'Recording' and 'Studio' have also found some fans. These employ most of the classic Les Paul traits with accommodations for low impedance and 'weight relief'.

As we go to print the Les Paul 'Pushtone' offers interchangeable pickups, and no doubt the expanding 'Digital' domain will eventually find favour.

This volume, however, pays service to the guitar that evolved in 1952–60, was deleted and subsequently resurrected and now continues a subtle evolution, a design classic in musical instrument history.

Ball-end – Conventional type of guitar string end.

'Biasing' – Setting the idle current in the power output valves of an amplifier. A valve is 'biased' by setting the amount of DC current flowing through it when no signal is present at the valve's grid with respect to its cathode. Increasing the bias determines the power output and the amount of distortion.

Bigsby – A patented vibrato device developed by the late Paul Bigsby.

Black Beauty – Nickname given to and now adopted for the black-finished Les Paul Custom guitar.

'burst – The popular nickname for the coveted '57–'60 sunburst Les Paul 'Regular' and 'Standard'.

Bumble Bee – Nickname for early Les Paul capacitors.

Capo – Abbreviation of 'Capodastro', originally a Spanish device. A clamp across the strings of a guitar, shortening the effective sounding length for musical transposition.

Carved top – Originally referred to the maple cap on many Les Pauls which emulated the carved-top profile of a violin. The carved top is now also seen on solid mahogany and veneered Les Pauls.

Dead spot – Spot in the machine head mechanism turn where no pitch-change is heard in the relevant string.

Earth loop (or ground loop) – A situation that arises when two pieces of equipment with earthed mains plugs are also connected by audio cables, effectively creating two paths to earth.

EQ – Equaliser.

Equal temperament – The name given to a system of dividing the chromatic scale into 12 exactly equal half-steps.

Feeler gauge – A gauge consisting of several thin blades, used to measure narrow spaces.

Flame – A type of maple grain found on some 'bursts.

FX – Effects.

Gotoh – Manufacturer of a bolt-on vintage-like machine head introduced in 1981.

Ground loop – See 'earth loop'.

Headstock angle – The angle between the neck and headstock, nominally 17° on most Les Pauls but sometimes less on '70s guitars; not thought overly critical even by Les Paul.

Headstock taper – Some early '50s Gibsons feature a tapered headstock profile though this was in decline by 1952, the year of the Les Paul's introduction.

Heat sink – A means of drawing heat away from areas adjacent to components that are being soldered, often achieved by the use of crocodile clips or similar.

Humbucker – Double-coil pickups wired in opposite phase and physically arranged in parallel or stacked to cancel induced low frequency hum. The electrics can be wired in series or parallel – series is the norm.

Kluson – Type of machine head used on many Les Pauls.

Long tenon – The neck joint employed on vintage and *some* reissue Les Pauls.

'Nashville stringing' – Modification in which a banjo G string was substituted for a guitar's E first string, the E string subsequently used as a second string, the B string as a first unwound 'plain' third, the normal wound third as its fourth string, and so on.

PA – Public address system.

PAF – A coveted decal applied to Gibson humbuckers from late '57, referring to the Patent applied for and granted in 1959 (patent number 2737842). Not present on the very first humbuckers and now used extensively on reissues.

Phase reversal – When the polarity of a DC circuit is reversed, often in the context of mixing polarities – *eg* one pickup 'in phase' the other 'reverse phase'. The ensuing phase cancellation produces interesting and unpredictable perceived equalisation effects, infinitely adjustable by volume control adjustment on the individual pickups. The most obvious effect is a cancellation of bass frequencies.

Pots – Potentiometers.

Quilt Top – A type of maple grain patterning on some 'bursts.

RF – Radio frequency.

Schaller – Type of machine head used on some modern Les Pauls.

Screen(ing) – Metallic shield around sensitive 'unbalanced' guitar circuits, connected to an earth potential to intercept and drain away interference.

Tune-O-Matic – A patented adjustable bridge developed for Gibson guitars in the mid '50s.

Volute – A neck reinforcement employed on some '70s Les Pauls.

VOS ('Vintage Original Spec') – A new guitar made as if of the model's original 'vintage' year of manufacture.

Wall warts – External DC power supplies.

Guitars

■ Most of the case study guitars were supplied by Peter Cook's Guitars, Hanwell, London (www.petercooks.co.uk), a good shop with a long-established reputation as well as knowledgeable, helpful staff and management.

■ The 'Robot', 'Digital' and Peter Frampton guitars were supplied by Jeremy Singer, UK PR Manager, Gibson, London.

Specialist tools and parts

Stewmac in the USA (www.stewmac.com) has virtually every specialist tool and part you could possibly need to maintain and repair your guitar. UK contacts include www.axesrus.com, www.gibson.com, www.wdmusic.co.uk and www.allparts.uk.com.

Historic guitar information

www.backbeatuk.com publishers of many superb guitar books, including *50 years of the Gibson Les Paul* by Tony Bacon.

Technical advice

Gibson's own website – www.gibson.com – carries a range of useful drawings and schematics on most Gibson guitars.

Lemon oil

D'Andrea, USA, from www.musicexpert.com.

Strings

www.djmmusic.com.

Plectrums

www.jimdunlop.com.

General tools

Draper – www.draper.co.uk.

My thanks to:

Lester Polfus, genius and inventor, for his generous time, anecdotes and stories. I can't imagine the music world without his timeless contribution.

John Diggins, for so much advice and technical expertise. John makes very sophisticated 21st-century guitars but has great respect for the classic luthiers' art in the Les Paul guitar.

The many very patient guitar techs who answered my questions, including Graham Lilley, guitar tech for Gary Moore, and Ron Eve for advice on Mark Knopfler's Les Pauls.

Mick Taylor, editor of *Guitarist* magazine, for advice and information.

Peter Cook's Guitar World, London, who made many of the featured Les Pauls available: Trevor Newman, Paul White, Rob West and Stuart Monks.

Jeremy Singer at Gibson UK, who not only supplied some guitars but assisted with much information and photographs.

Andy Tylee, who supplied the Les Paul Black Beauty and plays a mean blues harp.

Phil Beech of So '77, who loaned the '70s Goldtop and is still trying to wear it out.

David Wilson, publisher of *The ToneQuest Report*, for advice on Freddie King amplification.

Draper tools for the generous supply of the general tools required.

Andy Kerr for his 'Custom'.

Backbeat Publications – Nigel Osborne for interest, enthusiasm, and a magnificent series of great books and photographs.

Angela Meyer for locating some missing book pages.

Judy Caine – without whom I would get nothing done.

Karl Balmer, who puts up with Daddy making a noise and vanishing into his garret for hours on end.

Brendan McCormack of Mind Scaffolding Inc, a constant source of inspiration and provocation.

Zachary Fjestad at Blue Book Publications Inc for dating information.

Dave Gregory of XTC for guitar advice, the guitar loan, use of his studio for photography and, most importantly, for introducing me to the delights of early Goldtops.

Mike Robinson of My Rare Guitars.

Stewmac.com for parts and advice.

Julian Ridgway at Redferns Music Picture Library for his help and instant response to requests.

Sue Baker at Waukesha County Historical Society and Museum

Vanessa Ainsworth of Global Technologies Europe for untangling the Ethernet cable issues on the 'Digital' Les Paul.

The Vintage Guitar Gallery for potentiometer codes.

Richard Buskin for the 'Brothers In Arms' interview with Neil Dorfsman.

Mike Vernon for his generous contribution on his Peter Green recordings.

Stijn Vergeest at Gibson Europe Customer Service for Epiphone info.

Julian at Fake 58 for capacitor info.

Alex Semple at Seymour Duncan/Basslines/DTAR (5427 Hollister Ave, Santa Barbara, CA 93111-2345) for pickup information.

And the authors of the following publications:

Les Paul in His Own Words by Russ Cochran.

Gibson Guitars: Ted McCarty's Golden Era by Gil Hembree.

50 Years of the Gibson Les Paul by Tony Bacon.

Gibson Electrics: The Classic Years by A.R. Duchossoir.

The Seymour Duncan *Pickup Source Book*.

The Gibson Les Paul Book by Tony Bacon and Paul Day.

The Beauty of the 'burst by Yasuhiko Iwande.

Totally Guitar by Tony Bacon and Dave Hunter.

The Guitar Player Repair Guide by Dan Erlewine.

The Players' Guide to Guitar Repair by Dave Burrlock.

The Tube Amp Book by Aspen Pittman.

Jim Marshall, The Father of Loud by Jim Marshall and Rich Maloof.

PHOTO CREDITS:

Nigel Osborne – The Balafon Image Bank.

Clay Harrell of guitarhq.com.

R.G. Keen.

Stephen A. Hawkins – King Records.

Guy White – Snap Galleries Ltd.

Dave Brolan.

Epiphone Inc. for the use of their generous research archive.

Bill Fajen for 'Greeny' photographs (copyright 2006), with generous assistance from Phil Winfield. Jol Dantzig of Hamer guitars for further info on 'Greeny'.

Kettering General Hospital for CAT scan of the Peter Frampton Guitar.

Getty Images

John Pridmore – John Pridmore Studio

Credits

Author – Paul Balmer

Editors – Steve Rendle and Louise McIntyre

Design – Richard Parsons and Lee Parsons

Page build – James Robertson

Copy editor – Ian Heath

Technical advisor – John Diggins

Studio photography – John Colley

Technical and Macro photography – Paul Balmer

Photo research and administration – Judy Caine

"Now put down that
Allen key and wail!"

Paul Balmer September 2008